SPACE IS AWESOME!

101 INCREDIBLE THINGS EVERY KID SHOULD KNOW

ALICE HARMAN

ARCTURUS

Picture credits

p15tr: Nima Kasraie; p28tl NASA/Robert Markowitz; p33t U.S. Army; p33b Draper Laboratory, restored by Adam Cuerden; p34 NASA/JPL; p35tr National Astronomy and Ionosphere Center; p38 USGov-NASA; p39m NASA; p41b NASA; p42t NASA; p43m Maksym Kozlenko; p45b Johan Hagemeyer; p47m NASA; p52t Ken Crawford; p57b John Colosimo/ESO; p59b NASA/CXC/Huntingdon Inst. for X-ray Astronomy/G. Garmire, ESO/VLT; p65t Denys; p66t Smithsonian Institution; p73m The Yerkes Observatory; p102t NASA/ JPL-Caltech/MSSS; p106t NASA/JPL-Caltech; p107m N. Metcalfe & Pan-STARRS 1 Science Consortium; p109t NASA; p112b NASA, H. Ford (JHU), G. Illingworth (UCSC/LO), M.Clampin (STScI), G. Hartig (STScI), the ACS Science Team, and ESA; p113b University of Warwick/Mark Garlick; p114t ESA/Hubble & NASA Acknowledgment: Judy Schmidt; p115t NASA/ESA/Hubble Heritage Team; p115b NASA Goddard Space Flight Center; p117b ESO; p119t NASA/JPL-Caltech; p119b NASA/CXC/Stanford/I. Zhuravleva et al. All other images from Shutterstock.

ARCTURUS

This edition published in 2019 by Arcturus Publishing Limited
26/27 Bickels Yard, 151–153 Bermondsey Street,
London SE1 3HA

Author: Alice Harman
Editor: Becca Clunes
Designer: Sarah Fountain

978-1-78888-552-2
CH006565NT
Supplier 26, Date 0319, Print run 7963

Printed in China

What is STEM?

STEM is a world-wide initiative that aims to cultivate an interest in Science, Technology, Engineering, and Mathematics, in an effort to promote these disciplines to as wide a variety of students as possible.

Introduction

SPACE IS AMAZING!

From the Sun in the sky all day to the Moon and stars at night, space is a part of our everyday life. But sometimes we can take it for granted, rather than stopping to think about just how incredible it is! In this book you'll find 101 amazing facts about space—everything from animal astronauts and exploding stars to cannibal galaxies and diamond rain.

What does space smell like? Why could crying in space kill you? How does our atmosphere protect us from asteroids? All of these questions and many more will be answered in the pages of this book, so read on and open your eyes to the mind-blowing world of space!

YOU LIVE INSIDE THE SUN!

Earth is inside the Sun's atmosphere, the layer of gases that surround the burning star. In fact, the whole of our solar system sits within the Sun's atmosphere.

WARNING! LOOKING AT THE SUN, EVEN FOR A SECOND, CAN SERIOUSLY AND PERMANENTLY DAMAGE YOUR EYESIGHT. DON'T DO IT!

Layers of atmosphere

The Sun's atmosphere is made up of three layers. The layer closest to the Sun's surface is the photosphere, and it's so bright that usually it's the only part of the Sun we can see. Next comes the chromosphere. The gases in this layer get hotter and hotter as they move out, reaching around 9,700°C (17,500°F). But that's nothing compared to the outermost layer, the corona ...

FACT 2

The Sun makes up more than 99% of the mass of the solar system. Jupiter makes up most of the rest.

The mighty corona

The corona is around 200 to 500 times hotter than the chromosphere layer below it, reaching up to 3 million Celsius (5.4 million Fahrenheit). The corona stretches around 5 million km (3 million miles) into space, and then turns into the solar wind, the Sun's flowing atmosphere that stretches across the solar system. Earth is within the reach of this solar wind, but luckily it cools down a lot before it gets to us!

Magnetic power

The corona's extreme heat might be linked to the fact that the Sun is powerfully magnetic. Electric currents within the Sun create a magnetic field that affects our entire solar system. One of the things this field does is protect us from 90% of the deadly cosmic rays moving through space. The amount of radiation that makes it through to Earth is low enough not to cause us problems.

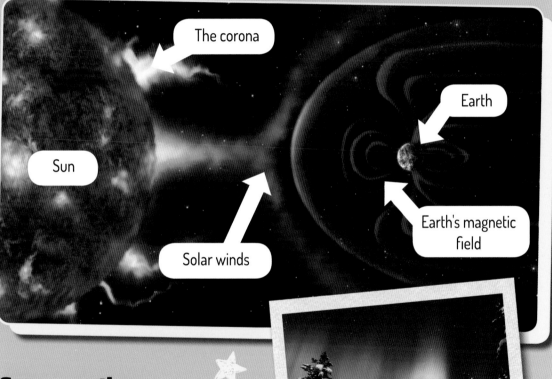

The corona

Earth

Sun

Solar winds

Earth's magnetic field

Space weather

Changes in the Sun's magnetic field, such as powerful magnetic storms, can affect us on Earth. The Sun shoots out solar winds, streams of speeding energy particles that can overcome Earth's own magnetic field and make our electronic objects stop working properly.

The Northern and Southern Lights occur when solar winds hit the Earth's atmosphere.

YOU ARE ALWAYS MOVING AT SUPER SPEED

Even when you're just sitting on the sofa watching TV, you're actually moving very fast! The Earth travels 970 million km (600 million miles) around the Sun each year.

Wheeeeee!!

Tied to the Sun

The Sun is much bigger than Earth, so it has much stronger gravity. The Sun pulls on Earth, so rather than Earth free-floating through space it is tied to the Sun and constantly travels around it in a set path. This is called Earth's orbit around the Sun, and it is more of a stretched egg shape than a perfect circle. The other planets in the solar system are also trapped orbiting around the Sun.

AROUND 1,300,000 EARTHS COULD FIT INSIDE THE SUN.

Spinning around

At the same time as Earth is moving around the Sun, it is also constantly spinning around. From here on Earth, it looks like the Sun is moving up and down and across the sky through the day. It's like when you look out of the window on a fast train and everything outside seems to be speeding past, but actually it is the train that is moving rather than anything outside.

Good night, Sun! We'll spin around and see you again tomorrow.

Star safari

As Earth orbits the Sun, it travels through different areas of space and we can see different stars. Earth always moves in the same direction around the Sun and at roughly the same speed, so we know which stars and other objects in space we will be able to see at certain times of the year.

FACT 4

If a human ran as fast as Earth moves around the Sun, they would finish seven back-to-back marathons in a single second.

Chain of orbits

The Sun does not stay still while Earth and the other planets in our solar system move around it. It orbits the middle point of our galaxy, the Milky Way, at around 230 km (143 miles) a second. The Milky Way orbits around a point between itself and the largest nearby galaxy, Andromeda. And our entire Local Group of galaxies orbits within a larger group called the Virgo Supercluster, which itself moves around other bigger structures. It's exhausting!

MORE THAN 1,300 EARTHS WOULD FIT INSIDE JUPITER

The Moon is a long way from Earth, around 384,400 km (238,900 miles). If you lined up all the planets in our solar system end to end, they could fit in the space between Earth and the Moon.

The little ones

The four inner planets in the solar system—Mercury, Venus, Earth, and Mars—don't take up very much space at all. Mercury is the smallest planet, and could fit inside Earth 18 times over. Scientists think that some of Mercury's surface might have been burned off when it was forming, because of it being so close to the Sun. Its huge liquid metal core makes up 75% of its total size, which is unusual for a planet.

Jump in Mercury, there's lots of room!

The frozen giants

It's a big jump in size from the inner planets to the outer frozen giants. Jupiter and Saturn are gas giant planets, while Neptune and Uranus are ice giants. Neptune and Uranus are around four times the size of Earth, but Uranus is a little bigger than Neptune. Neptune is a bit heavier than Uranus, though, because of the different materials in its core.

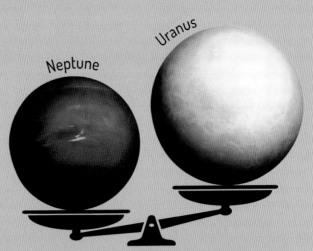

Neptune

Uranus

The big players

The planet taking up the most space by far in this line-up would be Jupiter. It is so big that all the other planets in the solar system could fit inside it with plenty of room to spare. Saturn is the second largest planet in our solar system and, like Jupiter, it is called a gas giant. Gas giants have a small, rocky core but are mostly made up of layers of liquid and gas.

Speeding through space

Despite the huge distance between Earth and the Moon, it only takes about three days for a spacecraft to travel there! A spacecraft has to be going very fast to break away from Earth's gravity and out into space—around 11 km (7 miles) a second, which means a speedy journey to the Moon. The Moon is working against us, though ... it's moving 3.82 cm (1.5 inches) farther away from Earth each year!

OUR HOTTEST PLANET IS NOT CLOSEST TO THE SUN

Mercury may be the closest planet to the Sun, but it's fiery Venus that takes the top hot spot in our solar system. The second planet from the Sun is a meltingly hot 462°C (864°F).

Hell on Venus

Venus can often be seen with the naked eye from Earth. Looking at this beautiful, bright planet shining in the sky, you'd never know how hellish it is down on its surface. As well as being burning hot, it also has such thick clouds of acid that almost no sunlight gets through, making it a dark and gloomy place. Add in its raging winds, wild storms, volcanoes, and crushing air pressure and it's not looking very appealing ...

I'm hot stuff!

FACT 7

Venus's hurricanes are over twice as fast as the strongest hurricanes on Earth.

Locking in heat

Venus's atmosphere, the layer of gases that surround planets, is mainly made of carbon dioxide. Venus is hot because of the "greenhouse effect" created by carbon dioxide, which traps a lot of the Sun's heat and only lets a small amount of it back out into space again. This is also happening on Earth and causing global warming.

Rays

Heat

Moon-like Mercury

Over on Mercury (below), it's a bit calmer than on Venus. In fact, it looks very much like the Moon! Mercury's surface is also rocky and covered with craters . Another similarity between Mercury and the Moon is that they both have only a very, very thin atmosphere. As the closest planet, Mercury gets a lot of heat from the Sun, but almost all of it quickly escapes back into space again.

Too hot and too cold!

It is still incredibly hot on Mercury at times, though. When it faces the Sun, Mercury's surface can reach 427°C (801°F)—almost as hot as Venus. But when it spins away from the Sun and night falls, the temperature can get as cold as -180°C (-290°F). The hottest and coldest temperatures ever recorded on Earth are 56.7°C (134°F) and -89.2 °C (-128.6 °F).

PLUTO IS ONLY HALF AS WIDE AS THE USA

Poor Pluto. It used to be considered the ninth planet in our solar system, but scientists have realized that it's just too small to be a real planet.

Days of glory

For 76 years, Pluto was part of an elite group—the planets of our solar system. First discovered in 1930, it was believed to be the most distant planet from the Sun. But in 2006 scientists decided it isn't a planet after all. It meets the first two "musts" of being a planet—circling a star (the Sun) and having enough gravity to pull itself into a round 3D shape—but fails the final test ...

THE LARGEST OF PLUTO'S FIVE MOONS, CHARON, IS SO BIG THAT IT MAKES PLUTO WOBBLE.

USA

Sun · Mercury · Neptune · Earth · Jupiter · Asteroid Belt · Mars · Saturn · Uranus · Venus · Kuiper Belt

Sharing space

Pluto hasn't managed to clear the area around it of other objects, which is the third thing a planet needs to do. It is part of the Kuiper Belt, an area of icy objects on the outskirts of our solar system, and it still shares its space with a number of other large objects. It is too small to have strong enough gravity to either trap large nearby objects in its gravity or to throw them out into space.

Tough decisions

There was a lot of global debate between scientists before Pluto was downgraded from a planet to a dwarf planet. If scientists had allowed Pluto to be considered a planet despite only meeting two out of the three standards, other objects in our solar system—including many moons —would also have to be considered planets. We could have ended up with dozens of official planets—that's a lot of names to remember!

Dwarf planets

At the moment, Pluto is one of five official dwarf planets in our solar system. Three of the other dwarf planets—Haumea, Makemake, and Eris—are near Pluto, in the Kuiper Belt. Ceres is the only dwarf planet in the asteroid belt, between Mars and Jupiter. Scientists believe there are many more dwarf planets in our solar system that we haven't yet discovered—up to 200 in the Kuiper Belt and 10,000 in the area beyond.

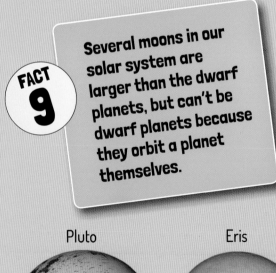

FACT 9

Several moons in our solar system are larger than the dwarf planets, but can't be dwarf planets because they orbit a planet themselves.

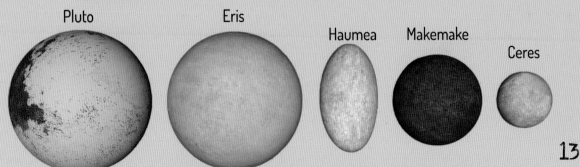

Pluto · Eris · Haumea · Makemake · Ceres

THE MOON MAY HAVE BEEN PART OF EARTH

Many scientists believe that the Moon is made from material chipped off the Earth when an object the size of Mars crashed into our young planet around 4.45 billion years ago.

Violent beginnings

That long ago, Earth would only have been around 50 million years old and the solar system would also only recently have come together. In these early stages, big crashes are very common. Many scientists think that the huge amounts of hot, rocky material blown off Earth by this crash got trapped by Earth's gravity and circled around the Earth, eventually clumping together to create the Moon.

The Big Splash theory

This Moon creation story is often called the "Big Splash" theory. It fits with some things we have learned about the Moon. Astronauts have collected rock samples from the Moon which are similar in some ways to rocks found on Earth. Also, the Moon doesn't have much iron compared to Earth, but most of Earth's iron is in its core so if the Moon is made of its rocky outer layer this would make sense.

This moon rock was collected during the Apollo 15 mission in 1971.

Earth's tilt

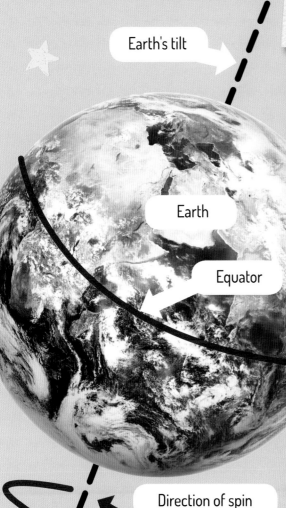

Earth

Equator

Direction of spin

Other Moon theories

It's important to remember that scientists do not always agree on a single theory, although often one idea becomes more popular than others over time. Some scientists still believe that the Moon is one huge chunk chipped off the Earth, rather than lots of bits of material that later joined together. Others think that it was a large passing object that was trapped in Earth's gravity when it got too close.

Tilted Earth

Imagine grabbing a pole in a fire station and swinging around and around on it in one direction. Earth constantly spins like this around its axis, an imaginary pole running through its middle. Except its axis doesn't stand up exactly straight—it tilts a bit to one side. It is widely thought that this is because when the large object hit Earth and created the Moon, the force of it also knocked the Earth permanently off kilter.

EARTH HAS A SECOND (MINI) MOON

The asteroid 2016 HO3 is circling Earth like the Moon we all know and love, and has probably been doing so for the last 100 years.

Get out! I'm the only real Moon.

Shhh, I just want a nice family picture.

EARTH'S MOON IS UNUSUALLY LARGE COMPARED TO OUR PLANET'S SIZE.

A sort-of moon

Asteroid 2016 HO3 is not exactly a true moon, as it drifts a little behind or ahead of Earth as it circles our planet. Another name for a moon is a natural satellite—it orbits around a planet like man-made satellites for weather and TV do. 2016 HO3 is a quasi-satellite—in other words, a sort-of moon—because it doesn't stick close enough to Earth.

Dancing with Earth

Although asteroid 2016 HO3 is around 100 times farther away from Earth than the Moon, and doesn't stick as closely to us, it definitely has a long-term connection to Earth. It will be with us for centuries to come. Other asteroids sometimes get trapped in Earth's gravity and, as NASA puts it, "dance with Earth" for a while, but only for a short time and then they are back off on their way.

The pattern 2016 HO3 makes when it circles the Earth is unusual.

No-moon mystery

Neither Mercury nor Venus has a moon. Mercury doesn't have a moon because it is so close to the Sun that its own gravity could never compete with the Sun's pull. It is more of a mystery as to why Venus doesn't have a moon. Many scientists think it's still too close to the Sun, some think its moon was destroyed, and others think that it "gave" Earth a moon. How generous!

FACT 12

Ganymede and Titan, Jupiter's and Saturn's largest moons, are both bigger than Mercury.

Many moons

Smaller planets tend to have few or no moons whereas larger planets can have huge numbers of them. Scientists think that Jupiter has 79 known moons in total, the highest number in our solar system, although only 53 have been officially named so far. Twelve of the planet's moons were only discovered for the first time in 2017.

FACT 13
JUPITER PROTECTS US FROM DEADLY COMETS

Some scientists believe that one reason we are able to live on Earth is because Jupiter's strong gravity helps to pull fast-moving comets away from Earth and throw them back out of our solar system.

Giant protectors

With Jupiter's help these really fast comets only hit Earth very rarely, every few millions or even tens of millions of years. Without Jupiter nearby, some scientists believe that comets would crash into Earth far more often. There are other scientists who think that Saturn also plays a big a role in protecting Earth, and that it's only the combined force of Jupiter's and Saturn's gravity which is strong enough to make a difference.

COMETS ARE MADE OF ICE, DUST, AND ROCK WHILE ASTEROIDS ARE USUALLY MADE OF METAL AND ROCK.

Leave my friend alone!

Thanks, Jupiter.

FACT 14
The first crash seen between two natural objects in space was Comet Shoemaker–Levy 9 hitting Jupiter in 1994.

Scars on Jupiter

Although Jupiter may play a role in protecting Earth from speeding comets, space objects such as comets and asteroids crash into Jupiter very often. When Comet Shoemaker-Levy 9 smashed into Jupiter, its pieces created dark scars on the planet's surface that were visible from Earth. In 2009 a dark spot the size of Earth was seen on Jupiter, believed to be damage caused by an asteroid only around 500 m (550 yards) wide.

Everyday scientists

Amateur astronomers—people who are not professional scientists but enjoy looking at and learning about space—have seen many objects crash into Jupiter in recent years. If seen in real time, this looks like a big "flash" of light, and the time it lasts tells us how large and heavy the object is. Amateurs' photos and videos are very useful, as professional telescopes don't always happen to be looking in the right place at the right time.

Asteroid crashes

While Jupiter often protects Earth from crashes, its strong gravity can sometimes work against us and send the occasional space object speeding in our direction instead—yikes! Some scientists believe Jupiter may have played a role in sending a huge asteroid to Earth 66 million years ago and killing off the dinosaurs, which let mammals grow and humans eventually evolve.

Dinosaurs may have been killed off by an asteroid crashing into Earth.

FACT 15

OUR SOLAR SYSTEM IS MIDDLE AGED

Our solar system is about halfway through its (very long) life. Scientists think our solar system began around 4.6 billion years ago and will survive for another 5 billion years.

Wow, that's an old rock!

This meteorite fell to Earth near Buenos Aires, Argentina.

Radioactive dating

So how do scientists know how old the solar system is in the first place? They can find out the age of ancient rocks and meteorites by looking at how radioactive materials in them have broken down over time. Radioactive materials give out radiation and break down very predictably, so scientists can work backward from their current state to tell their age. The oldest meteorites from our solar system that have ever been dated are 4.56 billion years old.

Running out of fuel

The Sun burns up its stores of hydrogen as fuel to survive. So far it has used about half of its hydrogen, so it has another 5 billion years' worth. Once it has burned up all this hydrogen, it will have to use its other materials for fuel and then it will begin to die.

A giant Sun

As the Sun dies it will get much, much bigger and hotter, becoming a red giant star. It will grow out to reach Earth, perhaps farther, probably destroying our planet as well as Mercury and Venus. Some scientists believe that Earth might instead be pushed out into space rather than burned up by the Sun. Either way, by this time Earth will be way too hot to support life.

Life after Earth

As the Sun grows into a red giant, and planets and moons farther out in our solar system grow warmer, life may be possible there for a while. As the Sun then shrinks and becomes a white dwarf, these planets will continue circling the Sun's cold, dim remains for a long time. Scientists are searching for planets outside our solar system that may be able to support human life in future.

FACT 16

LIFE MAY BE POSSIBLE ON OTHER PLANETS' MOONS

For a long time, scientists concentrated on finding other planets that may support alien life. Now, they are equally concerned about whether other planets could support humans.

Saturn and its sixth-largest moon, Enceladus.

Living on a moon

Jupiter and Saturn have lots of moons, and scientists believe that life may be able to evolve on some of them. We may think of our Moon as a cold, empty place compared to Earth, but if humans need to leave Earth in future, a moon might be our best option. With the help of advanced technology, we may be able to create an environment in which we can survive there.

FACT 17

Jupiter's moons Io, Ganymede, Europa, and Calisto are so big you can see them with just a pair of binoculars.

Moon oceans

Saturn's moon Enceladus and Jupiter's moon Europa both have liquid water oceans under their frozen surfaces. Saturn's moon Titan has an ocean of liquid methane (a gas on Earth) rather than water. Although scientists don't think this methane ocean could support any life forms familiar to us, it's possible that very different life forms could evolve in space and survive in this kind of environment.

Alien life

Scientists are hopeful enough about the possibility of life forms existing on Europa that a team once purposely destroyed a satellite heading toward Europa to stop it crash-landing and possibly hurting alien life. The Cassini spacecraft has recently explored Enceladus and found conditions in its oceans similar to those that we believe led to early life on Earth.

We don't know what aliens might look like, but it's unlikely they'll be like in the movies!

THE SEARCH FOR EXTRATERRESTRIAL LIFE IS OFTEN SHORTENED TO "SETI."

Better off on Earth

As far as we know, Earth is the only planet that is perfectly suited for humans to live on—as long as we treat it with respect. We need to stop global warming so we aren't forced off Earth before we have the technology to survive elsewhere. Positive change is possible! We've already shrunk the hole in the ozone layer—a part of our atmosphere that protects us from the sun's heat—just by stopping using certain chemicals.

FACT 18 CRYING IN SPACE COULD KILL YOU

Your eyes can form tears in space, but because there is no gravity the tears won't fall. They just make a big liquid bubble on your face. This can be very bad news ...

Dangerous tears

Andrew Feustel found out the hard way how risky crying in space can be. While he was on a spacewalk outside the International Space Station, a flake of the solution used to defog the inside of his spacesuit helmet got in his eye. It stung, so his eye reacted naturally and started watering to try to flush out the irritation. But crying doesn't work like that in space.

FACT 19 Astronauts wear normal clothes in space, and only put on a spacesuit when they walk outside the spacecraft.

Nooo, I can't see!

Blinded in space

As Andrew's eye pushed out tears, a liquid bubble formed and spread across his face and into his other eye. The tears stung painfully and meant he couldn't see anything at all, but there was very little anyone could do. Which is not what you want to hear when, as Andrew was, you are floating in space holding a power drill.

Happy ending

Luckily, after some time, Andrew eventually managed to move inside his spacesuit to rub his eye on a sticking-out piece of foam. He finished his spacewalk and returned safely to the International Space Station (ISS). Inside the ISS astronauts don't have to wear spacesuits with helmets, so although tears bubble on your face in the same way it's less of an issue as you can use your hands to brush them away. You can even watch them float in front of you!

WE HAVE TEARS IN OUR EYES ALL THE TIME TO KEEP THEM MOIST—THEY ARE CALLED BASAL TEARS.

Microgravity

The reason that tears do not fall inside or outside the ISS is not because there is no gravity. In fact, the ISS is so close to Earth that it still has 90% gravity. The reason is microgravity—the same reason you feel like you're flying just as a rollercoaster drops downward. As gravity pulls the ISS toward Earth, other forces pull it sideways, so rather than crashing down to Earth it free-falls around our planet in a constant circle.

FACT 20
SPACE SMELLS LIKE STEAK AND BURNING METAL

Astronauts agree that space smells ... funny. People describe it differently, but most agree that it is at once sweet, sharp, and metallic.

Bringing in a smell

Have you ever brought anything smelly into the house on your shoes? Don't worry, so have astronauts! Astronaut Don Pettit has said that his fellow astronauts carried in a "space smell" with them when they returned from spacewalks. Whenever he opened the hatch on the spacecraft to bring the astronauts back in, he noticed their spacesuits, gloves, helmets, and even their tools smelled odd—but it took him a while to figure out why!

SCIENTISTS BELIEVE HUMANS CAN RECOGNIZE 1 TRILLION DIFFERENT SMELLS.

Sugar and rotten eggs

Our solar system may be especially smelly. We have lots of carbon in our solar system and not much oxygen, giving it a strong and sooty smell. Think of an old car that gives off lots of nasty smoke from its exhaust—nice! We could have it worse—solar systems with lots of sulfur may smell like rotten eggs. On the other hand, it could be better, as scientists think some solar systems smell sugary sweet!

Eugh, who would have thought our solar system stunk like an old car?!

Astronaut smells

With up to six living, breathing human beings living aboard the International Space Station at any one time, things could get a bit smelly. Especially as no-one can have a shower or do laundry properly in space. There is a good built-in system for clearing smells but astronauts have said they sometimes got annoyed with each other for leaving sweaty workout clothes around and cooking smelly food!

Smell science

NASA has thought about trying to recreate the smell of space on Earth, talking to scientists about how they might be able to do this. The reason isn't just their curiosity—going into space is an exciting but often overwhelming experience, so in NASA's training programme they try to prepare people as fully as they can for their trip. This includes recreating sights, sounds, and maybe even smells.

FACT 21

You can't do laundry in space so dirty clothes are destroyed. They are sent down to Earth in a disposable spacecraft that burns up in the atmosphere, over the ocean.

SPACE TRAVEL CAN CHANGE YOUR BODY FOREVER

Astronaut Scott Kelly spent a year in the International Space Station. When he came back, scientists found that some interesting changes had taken place inside his body.

Scott and Mark Kelly

Twin astronauts

Scott Kelly has an identical twin brother, Mark, who is also an astronaut. As their DNA is almost identical, scientists can run some very interesting experiments looking at how each brother's DNA is affected by experiences in space. After Scott spent a year in space, many newspaper reports said his DNA had changed so much that he and Mark—who had remained on Earth—were no longer identical. It's a great headline but it's not quite right ...

FACT 23

Space can cause astronauts' eyes to change in ways that can cause vision problems and possibly even blindness.

Do I look different?

Switching genes

Genes are segments of our DNA, the code written into our body's cells that describe how we look and many other things about us. We inherit our genes from our parents, but different conditions or events in our lives can cause them to "switch" on and off and affect our body in different ways. What you eat, where you live, when you sleep, and all sorts of other things can trigger these on/off changes.

DNA strands

Permanent change

As you might imagine, going into space is quite an unusual thing for a person to do. However exciting it may be, it also puts a lot of physical stress on the body. It can cause genes to switch on and off, sometimes permanently so. While Scott was in space and Mark remained on Earth, Scott's genes switched on and off in different ways and it looks like around 7% of these changes are irreversible.

Bodies in space

Other changes are temporary— for instance, scientists found that Scott was taller than when he'd left, because the lower gravity in space meant his spine wasn't pulled down toward Earth as much. This happens to everyone in space, and they usually return to their pre-space height within ten days.

ASTRONAUTS CAN TIME TRAVEL

Time moves faster in space than on Earth because the Earth's orbit gives us an extra second per week. This means astronauts time travel as they move between space and Earth.

Space clocks

The existence of this extra time on Earth is called "time dilation" and it has been proven over and over again by taking very accurate clocks on trips into space. We can compare the time on two clocks—one in space and one on Earth—and see the difference between them. Scientists have also recorded the time difference between a pair of clocks after one of them had been in space.

I want my 100 millionths of a second back!

Einstein time

Famous scientist Albert Einstein "realized" that time isn't always the same—it depends on where you are. This isn't just true for space, though. Being higher up on Earth also means that you experience time as faster. If you spent your whole life at the top of a 100-floor skyscraper, you would lose around 100 millionths of a second of your life. Scientists have used clocks that are accurate to within one second over 3.7 billion years to show this on Earth.

Travel to the future

Russian cosmonaut Sergei Krikalev has spent more time orbiting around the Earth than anyone else—a total of 803 days, 9 hours and 39 minutes. This means he's completed more time travel than anyone else on Earth. As he still lives in the same time frame as everyone else on Earth, it is as if he has gone 0.02 seconds into his own future.

Science fiction

Along with invisibility and being able to fly, time travel is something that many people would love to do. But is it possible on a larger scale—days, months, years? Many scientists think so, although it's much more complicated to think about how to travel into the past than into the future. We are still only beginning to understand how things work differently elsewhere in space compared to on Earth, and what incredible things that might make possible.

A trip to the past? Maybe some day ...

YOUR PHONE COULD POWER THE MOON LANDING

Smartphones today are far more powerful than the supercomputers of the past which launched rockets into space in the 1960s and put men on the Moon.

Genius phones

A smartphone is an incredible piece of technology. It does the job of an address book, a calculator, an alarm clock, a map, a music player, a payment card, a bus ticket, and so many more things. It's not just a phone, it's a brilliantly fast and versatile computer that we carry around in our pocket—and it performs instructions hundreds of million times faster than the best computers used in the Apollo Moon missions.

Texting? Don't you know I could send you to space?!

Back in time

It's easy to forget that when we first landed on the Moon in 1969, the very first general-purpose programmable electronic computer had only been completed 23 years earlier. It was called ENIAC and the USA began building it during World War II. It eventually took up around 167 sq m (1800 sq ft) of space—that makes it the size of seven buses! It weighed around 30 tons, as much as five elephants.

Faster, stronger, smarter

By the time of the first Apollo space missions in the 1960s computers were more advanced, and they kept evolving over the following decades. As we moved into the new millennium, though, this rate of development kicked up to turbo speed. Technology has developed so quickly that even "smart" refrigerators and microwaves have more computing power than any of the computers NASA used to help put people on the Moon, let alone our smartphones!

Super programmers

The usefulness of a computer isn't just about its raw power, though—it depends on programmers working out how to give the computer its instructions. Margaret Hamilton, a NASA programmer on the Apollo missions, has said that it was like working in the "Wild West"—there weren't really many rules yet, they just had to make it up and try it! These programmers' genius and creativity helped harness the computers' limited power to do incredible things.

Margaret Hamilton and the software that powered the Apollo project.

WE HAVE SENT OUT MESSAGES FOR ALIENS

The Voyager I spacecraft was launched in 1977 with a solid gold record on board. It plays sounds from Earth and is intended as a friendly introduction for aliens who find it.

Introducing Earth

If you had to introduce an alien to life on Earth, which sights and sounds would you choose to give them the best possible understanding of our planet? The people responsible for the Golden Record had to decide exactly this. No pressure! A committee put together by NASA and headed by famous scientist Carl Sagan worked together to choose the contents—a selection of images, music, sounds from Earth, and greetings in different languages.

The Golden Record has a recording of a woman's brainwaves as she thought about subjects including history, the Earth's problems, and what it is like to fall in love.

Hello! We are from Earth!

Wie gehts?

Cover art

The record cover has a number of diagrams on one side, explaining where the spacecraft comes from and how the record can be played. As you would hope, NASA thought to include a record player on board so that any aliens can actually play it! There are also 115 images encoded onto the record itself—including photos of a city at night, heavy traffic on a road, and people eating or drinking in different ways.

One of the images on the Golden Record, showing people eating and drinking— a bit strangely!

THE GOLDEN RECORD IS DESIGNED TO STILL BE PLAYABLE A BILLION YEARS FROM NOW.

Earth sounds

Aliens playing the record will first hear a number of human greetings—starting in an ancient language called Akkadian and finishing in a modern Chinese dialect called Wu. The sounds of Earth include a human heartbeat, a baby crying, a train, and a dog barking. After this comes a 90-minute selection of music from all over the world—including classical Western and Eastern music, traditional songs from indigenous communities, rock 'n' roll, and the blues.

Swinging through space

The Voyager I (left) and Voyager II spacecraft were launched in the 1970s to take advantage of planets in our solar system lining up in a way that only happens every 176 years. The spacecraft used the gravity of each planet to swing to the next and eventually study our solar system's outer planets. After leaving our solar system they will travel through mostly empty space for a very long time—but we hope aliens may come across them some day ...

NEW PLANETS ARE DISCOVERED ALMOST EVERY DAY

Back in 1994, scientists Michel Mayor and Didier Queloz found a planet outside our solar system—but people didn't believe them for almost a year! Now we have found thousands, with more discovered all the time.

Exoplanets

An exoplanet is what we call a planet outside our solar system. Exoplanets circle around other stars, just as Earth circles around the Sun. Although no exoplanets were found until the 1990s, scientists had believed for years before this time that they existed. The reason behind this belief was that in understanding how planets formed around our Sun scientists realized that planets would similarly form around other Sun-like stars.

An artist's impression of 51 Pegasi b circling a star.

Too big

So if scientists believed in exoplanets, why did it take them so long to be convinced by the two scientists' 1994 discovery? Well, the issue was that this planet, named 51 Pegasi b—the first ever found circling around a Sun-like star—was just too big. The existence of an exoplanet this size didn't fit with scientists' ideas at the time about how planets were formed, so they thought at first that it must be a mistake.

I'm looking for a Goldilocks planet!

Goldilocks planets

The powerful telescopes available today help with spotting exoplanets. One focus of this search is finding "Goldilocks planets," named after the fairy tale. Like Goldilocks searching through the bears' house, scientists are trying to find a planet that is not too hot, not too cold, but just right for life to exist there.

FACT 29

The first evidence of an exoplanet was noted in 1917 ... but it was not recognized as a planet at the time.

Not the first

51 Pegasi b was the first exoplanet to be discovered orbiting a Sun-like star, but it was not the first exoplanet to be discovered. In 1992, Aleksander Wolszczan and Dale Frail found exoplanets around a type of tiny, fast-spinning star called a pulsar, which is the squeezed core left over after a massive star explodes.

FOOTPRINTS ON THE MOON STAY THERE FOREVER

There is no water or wind on the Moon to sweep away footprints on its surface. This means that astronauts' footprints may last as long as the Moon itself.

Walking on the Moon

Twenty-four people have flown to the Moon and twelve people have actually walked on its surface. The most famous are the first two to walk on the Moon's surface: Neil Armstrong and Buzz Aldrin. They flew there on the Apollo 11 mission, first stepping out onto the Moon on July 20, 1969. They spent over 21 hours on its surface, but less than three hours outside of the landing spacecraft.

FACT 31

The word astronaut comes from the Greek word "astron" (star) and "nautes" (sailor).

Just look at all these footprints!

38

Moon littering

It isn't just footprints that humans have left on the Moon. For a start, there are hundreds of pieces of spacecraft wreckage. Visiting astronauts have also left things behind, including two golf balls; 12 pairs of boots; empty food packets; 12 cameras (the films were brought back to Earth); and a single falcon feather dropped alongside a hammer to prove they would hit the ground at the same time.

NO ONE HAS EVER WALKED ON THE MOON MORE THAN ONCE.

Moon memorials

Other objects left on the Moon are meant to remain on its surface as symbolic reminders for all time. Some are to do with peace, such as a golden olive branch and a disk with messages of goodwill from leaders of 73 countries. Others are about space travel itself, including a 8.5 cm (3 inch) "fallen astronaut" sculpture that remembers those who have died for the cause of space exploration.

Surviving the Sun?

Although footprints and objects are not swept away by water or wind, they are also not protected from the Sun by Earth's atmosphere. The US flags left behind are bleached white from the Sun now, as is the family photo left on the Moon's surface by astronaut Charles Duke.

The Fallen Astronaut sculpture in front of a memorial plaque.

Charles Duke in front of a picture of himself walking on the Moon.

ASTRONAUTS CAN'T BURP IN SPACE

When people are in space, gas and liquids don't separate in their stomachs as they do on Earth. You can't burp without being sick!

No upside-down burping!

When you burp, you send gas from your stomach out of your mouth. You can do this without vomiting because gases are lighter than liquids and solids, so the gas sits at the top of your stomach. If you turned upside down and tried to burp, the gas would have risen upward toward your feet and so be in the wrong place. You would vomit instead of burping.

Uh-oh, guess I better hold it in until we're back home!

Soda bubbles

In space, though, astronauts experience what we call microgravity because they are in constant free fall toward Earth. Nothing is heavier than anything else in freefall, so gases don't rise above liquids or solids. Imagine a glass of soda. The bubbles within the liquid rush toward the top of the glass and escape, right? But in microgravity, the bubbles stay inside the liquid and don't move upward. The same thing happens with gas in your stomach in space.

In space, these bubbles would never reach the top!

FACT
33

Astronauts' feet get baby soft in space because they don't walk on the ground and so the rough skin falls off.

Astronaut Sunita Williams exercising aboard the International Space Station.

Floating liquids

Liquids are always moving through our bodies. When we are on Earth, gravity helps to move these liquids downward—in microgravity this doesn't happen, so the liquids rise toward the head. NASA found that over the year that astronaut Scott Kelly spent in space, around 2,000 ml (3.5 pints) of fluid shifted into his head.

Space workouts

Space travel isn't great for your health. Your body has to work quite hard against gravity when you're on Earth just to stay upright and move around, and in microgravity astronauts' muscles quickly waste away from not being used enough as they float around. To avoid this, astronauts have to exercise for around two hours a day.

PEOPLE THOUGHT ASTRONAUTS MIGHT GET SPACE DISEASES

When astronauts first went into space in the 1960s, scientists were worried that they might bring back deadly new diseases and tiny alien creatures.

HORNET + 3

The Apollo 11 astronauts, meeting President Nixon while still being kept in isolation.

I'M FINE, HONEST!

Moon sickness

When the crew of Apollo 11 returned to Earth after landing on the Moon for the first time, they were not allowed back out into the world for 21 days. They stayed in a secure area undergoing a range of different tests. Scientists had no idea what diseases or alien life forms they might have accidentally brought back with them, and didn't want to risk exposing Earth to new and mysterious dangers from space.

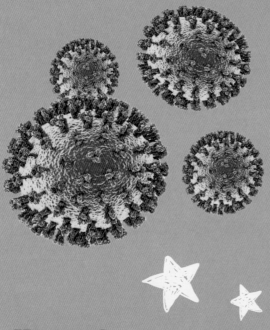

Sharing space

NASA's worries make sense—even between different countries on Earth, introducing new life forms can cause huge problems. Imagine what could happen with life from beyond Earth! When Europeans first came to the Americas, they brought diseases—such as smallpox and influenza—that killed many local people whose bodies had no resistance to them. Australia's plants and animals have also been badly affected by people bringing in species that do not naturally exist in the country.

Moon rocks

The Apollo crews also brought back quite a large amount of material from the Moon, and this could equally have carried dangerous or deadly life forms. NASA scientists kept the moon rocks in a secure space with different species of animals to make sure that they weren't poisonous or harmful in any way. They fed cockroaches moon rock and also used shrimp, oysters, and houseflies to test their safety.

A piece of rock from the Moon.

Safety first

The Apollo 12 and Apollo 14 crews (Apollo 13 wasn't able to land on the Moon) were also kept apart from others and tested in the same way when they returned to Earth. After this, scientists were convinced that there was no life on the Moon to attach itself to astronauts and pose a risk to life on Earth. People returning from space are now allowed to return home right away, after some health checks.

THE HUBBLE TELESCOPE SEES STARS BEING BORN

The Hubble telescope was launched in 1990 from the Discovery space shuttle. It travels around Earth taking incredible pictures of very, very far-off objects and events.

How far?

The Hubble telescope can see objects 13 billion light years away. A light year is the distance that light travels in one year—that's 9.5 trillion km (5.9 trillion miles), which is like looping around Earth 237 million times. Now multiply that by 13 billion—it's almost impossible to really imagine how far that distance really is!

Star birth as seen by Hubble

Quick, look! I think a star is being born!

THE HUBBLE TELESCOPE IS POWERED ENTIRELY BY THE SUN.

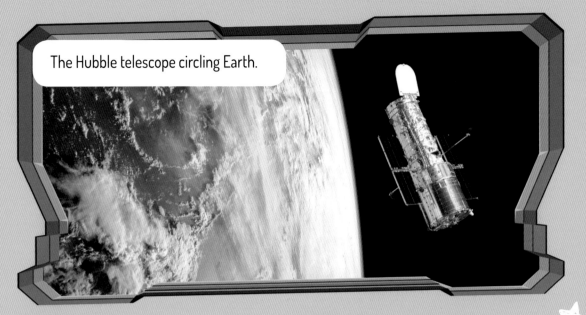

The Hubble telescope circling Earth.

Seeing clearly

Telescopes on Earth have to look through the clouds and gases of our planet's atmosphere to see out into space. This seriously limits how far they can see. In its position around 547 km (340 miles) above Earth, Hubble can see straight out into space without this hazy atmosphere getting in the way. This means it can see incredibly faint objects very far off into space.

Built for accuracy

In order to take pictures of such faint, distant objects, Hubble has to be incredibly accurate. It is built to keep very steady, which helps it to find an object and take a picture of exactly where it is. The amount to which it ever wavers its view to either side of an object is the same as about the width of a human hair seen from one mile away.

FACT
36

The telescope is named after Edwin Hubble, who discovered that there are other galaxies beyond our own Milky Way.

Perfect mirrors

The Hubble telescope uses a system of perfectly lined-up mirrors to see deep into space. These mirrors are incredibly precisely made to ensure that they can see things as accurately as possible. Hubble's main mirror is so finely polished that if you scaled it up to be as wide as the Earth there wouldn't be any bumps more than around 15 cm (6 inches) tall.

Edwin Hubble was a talented athlete and basketball coach, as well as a famous astronomer.

FACT 37

THE FIRST ANIMALS IN SPACE WERE FRUIT FLIES

Two fruit flies were launched into space in a rocket in 1947. The rocket just passed over the Karman Line 100 km (60 miles) up from Earth's surface, which is considered the start of space.

> This is one small flight for flies, one giant leap for flykind!

> There's no fruit in space, what are we going to eat?!

Flying high

As humans, we think pretty highly of ourselves compared with other animals. But despite all our cleverness, the humble fruit fly beat us into space! Scientists wanted to check how safe space travel was for humans, so they sent up two fruit flies in a rocket to see what happened to them. Luckily for the flies, they came safely back down to Earth and survived to buzz another day!

FACT 38

A number of animals have been bred in space, including jellyfish, frogs, and sea urchins.

46

Why fruit flies?

You wouldn't think that humans and fruit flies have a lot in common, but actually we're more similar than we look! Our genes contain information about our bodies and what they do, and over 60% of disease-causing genes in humans have recognizable matches in fruit flies. This means that looking at how fruit flies were affected by space travel could tell us quite a lot about what might happen to humans.

Weightless apes

Before humans went up into space, scientists were very concerned that we may not survive long periods of weightlessness. We share about 99% of our genetic code—our DNA—with chimpanzees, so in 1961 US scientists launched a chimpanzee named Ham into space to see how it affected him. He returned safe and well, just a little tired and thirsty. This mission paved the way for the successful first human astronaut launch later that year.

IN 1973, A SPIDER SPAN THE FIRST EVER WEB IN SPACE.

Animal heroes

Many other animals have been launched into space, including dogs, mice, rats, rabbits, insects, tortoises, fish, frogs, jellyfish, snails, and spiders. Sadly some of these animals did not survive, and we owe them a huge amount in helping us understand how to make space travel safe for humans. Scientists have continued to test how space affects animals in different ways and what long-term effects space travel might have on humans.

Ham, the chimpanzee astronaut.

A Russian stamp dedicated to Laika, the first dog in space.

THERE ARE AROUND 70 BILLION TRILLION STARS

If you counted up every single grain of sand in all the deserts and beaches on Earth, it would still be less than the number of stars in the known universe.

Stars and galaxies

In our galaxy, the Milky Way, there are more than 300 billion stars—that's 40 times as many as there are people on Earth. Scientists believe there are around 100 billion galaxies in the known universe. Some are much smaller than ours, but the total number of stars in the universe is so big it's hard to really imagine it.

I thought us stars were special?

Sorry pal, we're pretty common!

FACT 40

Using a basic telescope on a clear, dark night, you could see up to 2.65 million stars.

Seeing stars

Around 9,000 stars are bright enough for someone with average vision to see at night without a telescope or binoculars, but you can't see more than half the sky at any one time. This means that on a clear, dark night you could see an absolute maximum of around 4,500 stars. In most places the number will be much lower, though, as nearby night-time light—for example, from buildings and street lamps—drowns out the fainter stars.

A satellite image of light pollution at night.

Measuring brightness

The brightness of stars and planets is measured on a magnitude scale. The bigger the magnitude, the fainter the star is. On Earth the faintest stars we can see with the naked eye are magnitude +6.5, but with a small pair of binoculars you can see stars at magnitude +9. There are far more faint stars than bright ones, so using binoculars like this reveals up to around 108,000 stars across your half of the sky.

Galaxy gazing

Because Earth is at the end of one of our galaxy's four "arms," we can actually see the Milky Way in the sky. Except that most of us can't any more ... today, two-thirds of the world live in towns and cities that are too bright for people to see the Milky Way. Many countries now have International Dark Reserves, areas kept free from light pollution, to make sure we don't lose our views of space for ever.

The Alqueva Dark Sky Reserve in Portugal

FACT 41

Dung beetles can use the Milky Way to navigate.

NEUTRON STARS CAN SPIN 700 TIMES A SECOND

A neutron star is the tiny, dense core of a star that has collapsed in on itself. Just as an ice skater spins faster when they pull in their arms, so a star speeds up as it shrinks.

Packed in

Becoming a neutron star is one of the possible ways that a star's life can end. Neutron stars are incredibly dense, which means that they have a huge amount of matter crammed into a very small area. A neutron star packs around 1.4 times the mass of our Sun into a ball around the width of a small city.

Woah! That's a lot of spin!

Most of an atom is empty space.

No space

You are mostly made of empty space, and so is everything around you. This is because everything is made of atoms and over 99.9% of an atom is empty space. If you could remove all empty space inside the human body, every person on Earth could be squished inside an area the size of a sugar cube. A neutron star has had all its empty space crushed out of it, so only matter remains.

A pulsar.

Pulsars

There are different types of neutron stars, including strongly magnetic magnetars and extra-fast-spinning pulsars. From Earth, a pulsar looks like a star flashing on and off—it gives out two steady beams of light, but as it spins the beams go in and out of view. Jocelyn Bell Burnell first discovered pulsars in 1967, and the team of scientists studying them first thought they might be attempts by aliens to talk to us—they even named the first pulsar "Little Green Men 1!"

Star finales

A star only ends its life by exploding and turning into a neutron star if it is a certain size—too small and it becomes a white dwarf, too big and it collapses entirely into a black hole. Our Sun will become a white dwarf—when it runs out of fuel to burn, it will lose its outer layers and its hot core will slowly cool over a billion years or so.

It doesn't look little or green to me!

FACT 43

YOU CAN SEE INTO THE PAST

When you look at stars, you are seeing into their past. Because of how long light from stars takes to reach us, they may not even exist any more by the time we can see them.

Long-distance travel

Light travels incredibly quickly, almost 300,000 km (186,000 miles) in a single second. But many stars are so far away from Earth that it can still take a very, very long time for light to travel from where a star is to where we are.

Our photos of this spiral galaxy, M81, show it as it looked 12 million years ago.

I can't believe what I'm seeing!

FACT 44

If you moved at the speed of light, you could travel around Earth seven times in a single second.

Sun light

The Sun is by far the closest star to Earth, but light doesn't travel to us from the Sun in an instant—the journey takes around eight minutes. You must NEVER look at the Sun directly, because it can seriously damage your eyes and even leave you blind, but if you could you would be seeing the Sun as it looked eight minutes ago rather than right now.

Seeing the past

Other stars and planets are a lot, lot farther away than the Sun and so we are seeing much farther into their past. Scientists using powerful telescopes can see stars so far away that the light from them has taken billions of years to reach us. In this time, a star may have run out of fuel and ended its life—but we won't see this change for billions of years.

Dinosaurs on Earth

If there are aliens somewhere in the universe that are capable of seeing far into space, they will see Earth as it looked in the past—how far in the past depends on how far away they are from us. If they are far enough away that light from Earth takes 65 million years to reach them, they would see our planet as it looked in the time of the dinosaurs.

STARS ARE BORN IN GIANT GAS CLOUDS

A nebula is a huge cloud of dust and gases floating in space. Some of this dust and gas squashes together and heats up until lots of energy is created. The star is born and shines brightly.

Pulling together

So what makes a cloud of gas form itself into a star? Well, at first, gravity—the same force that pulls you down to Earth's surface. Gas particles are very weakly attracted to each other because of gravity, and as they come together the force of gravity then keeps pulling in more and more gas.

FACT 46

Horseshoe, Crab, Cat's Eye, Boomerang, Bubble, Ant, Tarantula, and Stingray are all real names of nebulae.

54

Some day I'm going to be a star!

Under pressure

As the gas cloud grows, the gravity squeezes it together and it gets hotter and higher-pressured. Eventually the pressure forces the cloud to start collapsing in toward its middle and it becomes a protostar. A protostar looks like a star but it is still forming, so it keeps pulling in gas and getting hotter and denser. This stage can last between 100,000 and 10 million years, depending how big a star is being formed.

Star birth

When a protostar's core is hot and pressured enough, the materials there change and give out a huge amount of energy. A star is born! It has begun burning its limited supply of fuel—when the fuel runs out the star will die, but it has billions of years before that happens.

I tried but I failed!

Failed stars

If a protostar doesn't manage to reach a big enough mass as it is forming, its core can't get hot enough to jump-start the reaction that turns it into a star. Instead, it settles into its new state as a brown dwarf. Brown dwarves are something between a giant gassy planet, such as Jupiter, and a small star. They create some light, like a star—but they have atmosphere with clouds and even storms, like a planet.

THE SUN IS A PRETTY AVERAGE STAR

The Sun is literally everything to us on Earth—we couldn't exist without it—but it's nothing special in the star world. There are stars a fraction of its size and others more than a thousand times larger.

The biggest

The Sun is huge in comparison to Earth, but not compared to other stars. The largest star that scientists are aware of today is UY Scuti, a red hypergiant that is more than 1,700 times the size of the Sun. If we could drop UY Scuti into our solar system in the Sun's place, it would swallow up everything out as far as Saturn.

FACT
48

Most stars that can be seen with the naked eye are bigger than the Sun.

Yeah well, everyone knows the best things come in small packages.

But wait ...

UY Scuti may take up the most space, but it has a much smaller mass than other stars. Interestingly, stars' sizes and masses do not always match up as you'd imagine—especially when it comes to giant stars. The star R136a1 is only around 30 times the size of the Sun but has 265 times its mass. UY Scuti is lightweight in comparison, with only 30 times the Sun's mass.

The smallest

The smallest star ever discovered is EBLM J0555-57Ab, and scientists think it is as small as a star can be. If a star doesn't get to a high enough mass as it is forming, it will become a brown dwarf rather than a star. EBLM J0555-57Ab is only a touch bigger than Saturn, which fits into the Sun around 1600 times over. It is a very faint star, around 2,000-3,000 times fainter than the Sun.

Alpha Centauri has two main stars and a third, fainter one tagging along too.

FACT 49

The closest stars to our Sun are over four light years away. They are a set of three stars called Alpha Centauri.

Lone star

The Sun does stand out from other stars in one way—it hasn't got any friends. Most stars have a companion star not too far away, and some are part of a system of three or four stars. Nearly all stars form with a companion, so scientists think the Sun might have lost its one at some point.

FACT 50

STARS HAVE STARQUAKES LIKE OUR EARTHQUAKES

Have you ever felt an earthquake? The ground shakes as the plates making up the Earth's outer layer shift around. Something similar happens on certain stars, but it's more powerful than an earthquake.

Mysterious magnetars

Starquakes take place on magnetars—small, very dense, strongly magnetic stars. A magnetar is a mysterious type of star—scientists have only ever identified 23 of them. It has by far the strongest magnetic field of any object in the universe, and scientists think it is the core that remains after a supermassive star dies.

FACT 51

A starquake sent out the brightest flash scientists have ever seen from beyond our solar system.

Earthquakes can cause huge damage as they tear through the Earth's crust.

Core and crust

Magnetars are so dense that scientists think at their centre there may be a hot, soupy core in which materials have been crushed into incredibly small particles. Around this core there is probably a thick, incredibly hot iron crystal crust that makes up most of the star's volume. The material deep inside this crust is called "nuclear pasta," and scientists think it is the strongest material in the known universe.

Ain't nobody stronger than me!

Bursting out

Scientists think that a starquake happens when a magnetar's magnetic field moves with so much force it rips through its crust. Apparently, the strongest material in the universe is no match for the incredible power of a starquake! The movement of the magnetic field also pulls the star's core like an elastic band, which eventually snaps—a fireball of particles and radiation shoots out of the rip in the crust.

FACT 52 Scientists have only ever recorded three starquakes—in 1979, 1998, and 2004.

A starquake in action

High energy

A starquake gives out a giant blast of energy so violent that one can affect us on Earth when it happens on a star 50,000 light years away. In 2004, a burst of energy from a starquake disrupted radio and submarine signals, took satellites offline, and actually moved the Earth's magnetic field. Luckily, it only lasted for a tenth of a second!

FACT 53
A BLACK HOLE CAN TEAR APART A STAR

In 2018, for the first time ever, scientists were able to watch an enormous black hole grab a star with its powerful gravity and shred it apart.

Black holes

A black hole forms when a large star dies and collapses in on itself. It has a huge mass in a small space, and its gravity is incredibly strong. In fact, a black hole's pull of gravity is so great that it creates a one-way system into itself—it draws in objects and light, which can then never escape.

FACT 54
There is a black hole, named Sagittarius A, in the middle of our galaxy.

Yikes!

Mwahahahaha, you can't get away!

Finding proof

Scientists have believed for a while that black holes are capable of destroying stars caught at their edge. They worked out that this would create an enormous blast and send a jet of matter shooting out across space at great speed. In 2018, they actually saw the jet, confirming their theory.

Seeing the invisible

Because no light can get out of them, black holes are invisible to us. Scientists use powerful telescopes and special equipment to find them in space. They look at how stars and other matter in an area of space move—when there is a black hole they spin around it and create a flat disk. The spinning matter gives off different types of radiation that scientists can record.

Don't panic!

A black hole sounds terrifying—invisible, destructive, with enough power to tear apart a star. But it doesn't zoom around the universe looking for its next kill and although it has very strong pulling power it can't suck in stars and planets from anywhere in space. A black hole can only destroy a star that passes very close to its edge.

FACT
55

Until 1967, black holes did not have one set name—scientists called them different things, including "collapsar" and "frozen star."

I'm panicking!

YOU ARE MADE OF STAR DUST

Most of the basic materials that make up our bodies were formed in stars over billions of years and journeyed across the universe when stars exploded.

> That's where we come from.

Human elements

An element is a material that cannot be broken down into any simpler substance. The human body is mostly made up of four elements, which are oxygen, carbon, hydrogen, and nitrogen. We also contain smaller amounts of many other elements, including calcium, sodium, chlorine, copper, tin, iron, and zinc.

The stuff of stars

Scientists can work out what a star is made of by looking at the light that it gives out. Every element within a star gives out light of a different wavelength, so by measuring the bright and dark patches of a star's light scientists can work out which elements it contains. Scientists have found that humans and stars share almost all of the same elements, although not in the same amounts.

Zinc is one of the elements that makes up both our galaxy and our body.

Multiple lifetimes

When certain stars approach the end of their life, they push out most of their mass in a huge explosion called a supernova. This matter is then recycled to create new stars, which eventually go supernova too and continue this cycle.

The Big Bang

Scientists think it is also possible that some of the hydrogen in our bodies actually came from the Big Bang—the huge explosion that created the universe. In the early days of the universe only the very lightest elements, hydrogen and helium, existed—they still make up 98% of the universe today. Over time, stars created other, heavier elements by squeezing atoms together in their hot, high-pressure cores.

First stars appear: 13.5 billion years ago.

The Big Bang: 13.7 billion years ago.

Formation of our solar system: 4.6 billion years ago.

THE UNIVERSE ISN'T MAKING MANY NEW STARS

Scientists believe that half of all the stars that have ever existed were created between 9 and 11 billion years ago. The rate of new stars being born has fallen hugely since then.

Slacking off

An international team of scientists found in 2012 that since the universe's star-making peak 11 billion years ago it has really been slacking off. The star birth rate has dropped by 97% from that peak to its current slump today. If this same trend continues, it will mean that 95% of all stars that will ever exist in the universe have been born already.

The Pillars of Creation is an area of space that has birthed many new stars, but it may be well past its peak now.

Hi-tech study

The team of scientists who made this discovery used three advanced telescopes to collect around ten times as much information as any previous similar study. They looked at a range of star-making galaxies at different distances from Earth, and were able to work out how quickly stars were forming at various points in the universe's history by measuring the light from clouds of gas and dust in these galaxies.

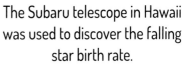

The Subaru telescope in Hawaii was used to discover the falling star birth rate.

Life cycle of a star

Stellar Nebula

Average Star

Red Giant

Planetary Nebula

White Dwarf

Massive Star

Red Supergiant

Supernova

Neutron Star

Black Hole

A star's life depends on its size.

Healthy galaxy

Many of the universe's billions of galaxies may no longer be forming stars, but our galaxy—the Milky Way—is in pretty good shape. Lucky us! As one of the universe's healthy, star-birthing galaxies, the Milky Way will play an important part in the universe's future.

Why so slow?

We are not sure why the star birth rate has slowed so much over time, but a 2017 study suggests that magnetic fields might be to blame. Scientists created a computer simulation of a particular galaxy—using all the known information about it to make their model as accurate as possible—and found that magnetic forces in the middle of the galaxy stopped its clouds of dust and gas from collapsing and forming stars.

FACT 58
EXPLODING STARS CAN OUTSHINE ENTIRE GALAXIES

When a star explodes at the end of its life, it is called a supernova. A supernova gives out a huge amount of light, which can sometimes be seen from Earth.

FACT 59
Scientists recently discovered a star lost in the glare of a supernova for 21 years.

A-maz-ing!

Supernova spotting

Around 1,800 years ago, scientists in China spotted a very bright star that didn't move, as they knew comets do, and that took around eight months to fade. This seems to be the first record of anyone seeing a supernova. The last sighting was a while ago now—back in 1604, when William Shakespeare was alive! This supernova is named after Johannes Kepler, a scientist who spotted it but mistook it for a new type of star.

Wow, kind of puts the Sun to shame ...

One every second

There is a supernova somewhere in the known universe roughly once every second. Count to ten slowly ... that's ten stars that have exploded in a violent blaze of light! There should be a supernova in our galaxy, the Milky Way, every 50 years or so—but they are tricky to spot. There was one visible from Earth 100 years ago but from historical records of the time it doesn't seem like anyone saw it at all.

FACT
60

A supernova can give out more light than our Sun does in its entire lifetime.

Supernova pretenders

Sometimes stars undergo explosions but aren't actually destroyed by them, as they would be in a supernova. During this type of event, a star gives out a huge amount of energy and becomes much brighter for a short time, before returning to its previous state. The huge amount of light given out is easily mistaken for a supernova.

Watch a star explode

There is due to be a supernova in 2022 that should be visible from Earth with the naked eye. This is the first supernova that scientists have said will happen within a set time period—in the past, they haven't been so confident of knowing exactly when one will take place. When the star system explodes it will become more than 10,000 times brighter, and stay bright for most of the next year.

FACT 61 SOME PLANETS HAVE TWO SUNS

More than half of all star systems in the known universe circle around two stars rather than one. Can you imagine having a second sun in the sky?

FACT 62 Scientists have found planets with three suns and one giant planet with four suns.

Strange as fiction

Our solar system has one Sun, but more than half of all solar systems in the known universe circle around two stars. Planets that circle around two stars are officially called "circumbinary planets" but sometimes they are also known as "Tatooine planets"—after Luke Skywalker's home planet in *Star Wars*, which famously has two suns.

Two suns? At least I remembered enough sunglasses!

Changing journeys

We move regularly around the Sun—one journey all the way around takes 365 (and ¼) days, an Earth year. (We have a Leap Year every four years to make up the quarter-days.) But for planets with more than one sun, it isn't so simple. Their movement is much more irregular and their journey time—and sometimes even their path—around their suns varies.

Hard to find

The Kepler space observatory, which looks for Earth-size planets orbiting other stars, has found a number of planets with two suns. But it's not easy—because of their irregular movement, scientists find it quite tricky to spot these planets. They search for small dips in a star's brightness, as these suggest that a planet could be passing in front of it and blocking a little bit of its light.

In the Kepler-47 system, two planets move around two suns.

Rare planets

Although most star systems have more than one star, it is quite rare for a two-star system to have any planets moving around it. The Kepler space observatory has found 2,600 planets beyond our solar system, but only 11 of them circle around more than one star. Scientists think that the magnetic force of the stars may hurl planets away from them, out of orbit.

The Kepler telescope was launched into space aboard a rocket in 2009.

FLYING THROUGH THE ASTEROID BELT IS EASY

Movies and TV shows often show spacecraft struggling to fly through areas with lots of asteroids, dodging between huge speeding rocks. The reality is much less exciting.

Asteroid belt

Asteroids are rocky objects, leftover bits and pieces from when the solar system formed billions of years ago, which still circle around the Sun. In our solar system, between the planets Mars and Jupiter, there is an area of space containing millions of asteroids. This is known as the asteroid belt, and most of the asteroids in our solar system are found within it.

Saturn

Jupiter

Asteroid belt

Mars

Earth

What?!
I was expecting
a challenge!

Venus

Space between

Although there are lots of asteroids to avoid, there is typically around 1 to 2.9 million km (620,000 to 1.8 million miles) between each one. It's difficult to even get close enough to an asteroid to see it as you're flying through the belt, let alone having to constantly dodge around them! You really have to aim at a particular asteroid in order to be sure of seeing one.

This is a disappointingly boring flight.

Not all alike

The largest known asteroid, Vesta, is 578 km (359 miles) wide, although most are much smaller than this. Asteroids are made of rock and metal, and the different types and amounts of the materials that make them up change how they look. For example, asteroids that contain lots of metal are shiny.

Beyond the belt

Although most of the asteroids in our solar system are found in the asteroid belt, there are some in other areas too. For instance, Trojans are what we call asteroids that circle around Jupiter. A number of asteroids pass close to Earth, and are known (a bit unimaginatively) as Near-Earth Asteroids—the ones that might be dangerous for Earth are the "Earth-crossers," asteroids that actually cross Earth's path and so could crash into us!

COMETS ARE DIRTY SPACE SNOWBALLS

A comet is made of a mixture of frozen gases and water ice with bits of rock and dust stuck in it. These materials come from the time when our solar system was formed.

Gas tail

Dust tail

Icy core

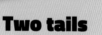

Who are you calling a dirty space snowball?

Two tails

Comets are made up of an icy core and a trailing tail. In fact, most comets have one blue tail made of gas and another brighter tail made of dust. It is the Sun's light hitting the dust particles in this tail that makes it shine so brightly. As the comet moves closer to the Sun, the sunlight pushes these dust particles back away into a long tail that can stretch for almost 10 million km (6 million miles).

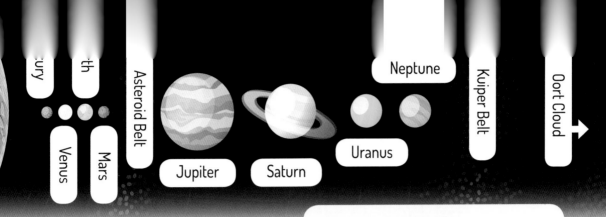

th

Venus

Mars

Asteroid Belt

Jupiter

Saturn

Uranus

Neptune

Kuiper Belt

Oort Cloud

The Kuiper Belt

Comets in our solar system come from one of two places—the nearest one to us is the Kuiper Belt. This is a huge, disk-shaped area that begins close to Neptune and continues past Pluto, containing many different icy objects. The comets that come from the Kuiper Belt are short-period comets, which take less than 200 years to circle around the Sun.

The Oort Cloud

The Oort Cloud is around 100 times farther away than the Kuiper Belt, running all around the edge of our solar system like a giant shell. No one knows for sure how many objects there are in the Oort Cloud, but it may be around 2 trillion—around 266 times as many people on Earth. Scientists think that long-period comets, which take longer than 200 years to circle around the Sun, come from this area.

A photo of Halley's Comet, taken in 1910.

Star finales

The most famous comet (for people on our planet, at least!) is Halley's Comet. It takes around 75 years to circle all the way around the Sun, and we can only see it at one certain point in this journey. Seeing the comet is a once-in-a-lifetime event for all but the very luckiest people. It was last visible from Earth in 1986 and may be able to be seen again in 2061. Don't miss it!

I've been waiting for years to see this comet!

73

FACT 65

A HUGE CLOUD OF WATER FLOATS THROUGH SPACE

Scientists have found a cloud far off in outer space that holds 140 trillion times the water in the Earth's oceans. It is the biggest amount of water that we have identified.

How much?

140 trillion is such a huge number that it's hard to even imagine how big it really is. Think about it this way—if you counted out 140 trillion seconds, it would take more than 4 million years! Our galaxy, the Milky Way, has a few large clouds of water, but this giant is around 4,000 times bigger than any of them.

I feel so small ...

FACT 66

Most of the water in our galaxy is in the form of ice.

Old water

Scientists believe that this area of water is around 12 billion years old—to give an idea of just how old that really is, the universe only came into existence around 13.8 billion years ago. This means that water was one of the first materials ever created. Before the cloud's discovery, scientists thought that water was first created around a billion years after we now know it was.

Finding the cloud

This cloud is so far away from Earth that it has taken light from where it is in space around 12 billion years to reach us. Light travels faster than anything else in the known universe, so that's a pretty long way away! Amazingly, we have developed such powerful telescopes that scientists were able to discover the cloud using two of them in Hawaii and California.

Black hole

As if being a universe-wide record breaker for holding water wasn't dramatic enough, this giant cloud also surrounds a huge black hole! This black hole has 20 billion times the mass of the Sun and it is part of a strange, giant object called a quasar that gives out a huge amount of energy.

This telescope in Hawaii has a pretty beautiful view of Earth, too!

ASTEROIDS CAN HAVE THEIR OWN MOONS

Some of the bigger asteroids in our solar system have moons of their own. In 1993, a tiny moon was spotted for the first time circling the asteroid 243 Ida.

Hi, Galileo, I'm 243 Ida and this is my moon, Dactyl!

Dactyl

The name of 243 Ida's moon is Dactyl. It is only 1.6 km (1 mile) across, almost 20 times smaller than the asteroid. Dactyl moves quite slowly, circling 243 Ida at around 36 km (22 miles) per hour, which is only a bit faster than a person sprinting. Although Dactyl is pretty small and slow, it's still an impressive record-breaker— the first moon of an asteroid ever discovered and photographed.

Galileo spacecraft

Dactyl was discovered by the Galileo space mission in 1993. The Galileo spacecraft was launched—with no one aboard—in 1989. It was the first spacecraft to explore Jupiter and its moons for a long period of time, circling around Jupiter for eight years. It took many pictures and measurements, teaching us more about this huge planet and its moons, but it also studied and photographed asteroids.

Not so special

Since this first sighting of an asteroid with a moon circling around it, scientists have discovered several more asteroids in our solar system that also have moons. In total, we know of more than 200 asteroids—both within and beyond our solar system—that have moons. In fact, there are asteroids that have more than one moon. A huge asteroid called 3122 Florence, which came pretty close to Earth in 2017, has two moons.

Scientists think that Jupiter has at least 79 moons!

Dwarf planets

We know that some planets have moons, and that asteroids can too, but what about another player in our solar system—dwarf planets? Well, Pluto may have been downgraded from a planet to a dwarf planet in 2006, but of the dwarf planets it is both the biggest and has the most moons—five! Haumea has two, Eris and Makemake each have one, and Ceres—which lies in the asteroid belt between Mars and Jupiter—doesn't have a moon.

PLUTO, 5 moons

HAUMEA, 2 moons

MAKEMAKE, 1 moon

ERIS, 1 moon

CERES, 0 moons

FACT 68

EARTH DESTROYS A CAR-SIZED ASTEROID EVERY YEAR

About once a year, an asteroid the size of a car hits Earth's atmosphere—the mix of gases that surround our planet. This creates an impressive fireball, which burns up before reaching Earth's surface.

50 rhinos a day

Every day, more than 100 tons of material—roughly the combined weight of 50 rhinos—falls from space toward us. Although this is a lot of material, the individual pieces aren't normally very big. In fact, it is largely space dust and objects smaller than a grain of sand. Most of it burns up as it enters Earth's atmosphere, the layers of gases around our planet.

> Wheeeee!

FACT 69

Asteroids aren't that big, in space terms. If you rolled together all the asteroids known in our solar system, they would only make up 4% of the Moon.

Burning up

When objects travel through space, they can reach very high speeds. When they hit the Earth's atmosphere at this speed, they squash the gas particles in the atmosphere in front of them as they go. A gas that gets squashed like this gets hotter. This makes the object heat up too, until it gets so hot that it burns up.

A space capsule re-entering Earth's atmosphere, its heat shield glowing red-hot.

Shuttle safety

When spacecraft return to Earth from space, they obviously have to re-enter our planet's atmosphere. So why don't they burn up like the other objects falling to Earth from space? Well, if we're not very careful, they do. Obviously we don't want that—especially if there are people on board. Spacecraft either have special insulating tiles to stop them getting too hot or they have a heat shield designed to melt away and carry off the heat.

Danger from beyond

Some objects are big enough that they burn up a bit when they hit Earth's atmosphere but not entirely. Usually the remains that hit the Earth are very small and don't cause a problem. But if an asteroid more than 1 km (0.62 miles) across hit Earth's atmosphere, it could have a global impact. There are asteroids in our solar system big enough to wipe out life on Earth, but they are too far away to be a danger.

An asteroid? Yikes!

SHOOTING STARS ARE NOT STARS AT ALL

Meteors are often called "shooting stars" because they look like bright stars moving across the sky, but they are not stars at all.

Not a star

A star appears as a still point of light in the night sky, and a meteor appears as a fast-moving streak of light. But although a meteor looks like a speeding star, they are actually very different. A star is a huge ball of burning gas far off in space, whereas a meteor is the glowing path of a small piece of rock or other matter that has entered Earth's atmosphere—the layers of gases that surround our planet—from space.

Yeah, not bad for a load of rocks and gas balls.

It's so beautiful ...

Burning bright

This small piece of rock or other matter from space, usually between the size of a grain of sand and a boulder, is called a meteoroid. When it hits Earth's atmosphere, it gets so hot that it burns up and changes into a gas. This burning gives off light, like a fire does, and we can see its visible path across the sky as a bright, glowing streak—which we call a meteor.

Meteorites found on Earth

Meteoroids, meteors, meteorites?

So now we know that a meteoroid is an object and a meteor is the light that it gives off as it burns up, let's look at meteorites ... Basically, if any part of an object from space makes it down to Earth's surface without burning up entirely in its atmosphere, it's a meteorite! It can be the leftover part of a meteoroid, an asteroid (which is bigger) or a comet (which is icy).

FACT
71

Meteor showers that are especially intense are called meteor storms. During these events, you could see more than 1,000 meteors in an hour!

Meteor showers

If you've ever been lucky enough to see a meteor, you'll know how special it feels to watch it zipping across the sky. Now imagine if you could see 100 of them in an hour! Meteor showers happen when lots of small objects fall into Earth's atmosphere at once, meaning that for a certain length of time—usually several days—there are lots more meteors to spot than normal.

SCIENTISTS LANDED A SPACECRAFT ON A COMET

In 2016, for the very first time ever, a team of scientists managed to successfully land on the surface of a speeding comet. That's some careful driving!

Can't you stay still for a second?! This is really hard!

Rosetta, Philae, and the comet

The lander that actually touched down on the comet was called Philae, and it was part of Rosetta, a larger spacecraft that had been following the comet for around two years. Rosetta launched in 2004 but took 10 years to arrive at its target comet. This comet, called 67P/Churyumov–Gerasimenko, is named after the two scientists who first discovered it in 1969.

FACT 73

Earth was often hit by comets early in its life, and scientists believe they may have given us some of the water for our oceans.

Moving target

67P/Churyumov–Gerasimenko is around 4 km (2.5 miles) across, which sounds quite big but as it travels at up to 135,000 km (84,000 miles) an hour it's not an easy target on which to land. Imagine it by thinking of trying to land on an area the length of Central Park in New York, while Central Park is moving at more than 300 times the speed of the fastest car in the world.

Bumpy landing

As Philae dropped down toward the comet, it took close-up photographs to help scientists understand more about comets. Unfortunately, Philae's landing wasn't a smooth one—it bounced twice and ended up in a shadowy area, where its solar batteries couldn't get enough light to charge up properly. In July 2015, as the comet passed nearby the Sun, it woke up again but soon ran out of power once more.

Philae landing craft.

Mission end

The Philae lander is still attached to the comet, and scientists hope that it may still send back more photos in future. For the Rosetta spacecraft, however, the end came in September 2016 when it crash landed into the comet. This was a planned end to the mission, as the comet is heading out into the outer reaches of our solar system. There isn't enough sunlight out there to continue powering Rosetta to fly through space with it.

That comet can't hurt me now!

FACT
74

In 1910, Earth passed through the tail of a comet. Some people were so scared about its possible effects, that they bought "anti-comet" umbrellas!

HUMANS ARE LEAVING JUNK IN SPACE

There are more than 17,000 man-made objects circling around Earth—and these are only the ones large enough to be tracked.

Bits and pieces

We think there are around 170 million smaller pieces of space junk, too, from paint flakes to nuts and bolts. Even the very tiniest objects can damage spacecraft. Bigger objects can be very dangerous if spacecraft crash into them because they are moving so fast—faster than a speeding bullet— as they circle around the Earth.

Come on guys, clean up after yourselves!

84

No longer needed

There are more than 1,400 working satellites circling around Earth, but there are also lots of old satellites that aren't in use any more. There are many pieces of burned-out equipment used to launch missions into space, left behind over 60 years of exploring space. There is a risk of this space junk crashing into working satellites and damaging them.

One of the many satellites circling Earth.

Chain reaction

Every time pieces of space junk crash into each other, more bits can break off and increase the total number of unwanted objects floating around Earth. If objects have any leftover fuel or batteries, they may also explode and send out lots of smaller bits. The only way to control the amount of junk circling around Earth is to remove the larger items.

Clearing up

RemoveDebris is a small, experimental satellite sent out into space to try out clearing up some of this space junk. In 2018 it caught its first piece in a test run—it sent out a target, which it then recaptured in a net, and the satellite and space junk fell back to Earth to burn up in the atmosphere. A net seems like a strangely simple idea, but it seems to do the job!

Space junk crashing into the International Space Station could be very dangerous for the astonauts on board.

MOST METEORITES ARE SMALLER THAN AN ORANGE

Every day, tons of meteorites reach the Earth's surface. But don't worry too much about getting hit by one on its way down—each one is usually tiny, no more than a speck of dust!

What is a meteorite?

A meteorite is an object that has come from space and crossed through Earth's atmosphere, the layers of gases that surround our planet, before landing somewhere on its surface. It was originally part of a larger (but still relatively small) object, which burned up as it hit Earth's atmosphere until only this small bit remained. This larger object may itself be a broken-off piece of an asteroid or a comet.

FACT 77
Meteorites have been spotted on the surface of Mars and other planets.

The orange looks tastier!

86

A meteorite falling into the ocean.

Where do they land?

Over 70% of the Earth's surface is covered in water, so it makes sense that most meteorites end up landing in the water rather than on land. They fall randomly all over the world, but it is easiest to spot and collect the ones that have landed in desert areas—both hot, sandy deserts and cold, snowy areas such as Antarctica.

Crashes and craters

If a meteorite is big enough, it creates a visible crater when it crash-lands. A crater is a bowl-shaped dip in the ground, with a raised ring around its top edge. There are fewer than 200 impact craters on Earth, but the Moon has thousands all over its surface. Earth's atmosphere slows down and burns up falling objects, but the Moon gets the full impact of any crash landing.

FACT 78

Dust in your home contains tiny burned bits of meteorite.

Not just meteorites

Asteroids and comets can also crash-land on our planet's surface. Like meteorites, they will partly burn up as they pass through Earth's atmosphere, but what survives and hits Earth can be much bigger than any meteorite. This means that they can create much bigger craters, and even have a worldwide impact—scientists believe an asteroid hitting Earth led to the dinosaurs dying out.

This impact crater was made almost 50,000 years ago.

FACT 79

TOYS ARE FLYING THROUGH SPACE RIGHT NOW

When NASA launched the Juno spacecraft in 2011, there were three special guests on board ... They are circling around Jupiter, farther away from Earth than any human has ever been.

Hi-tech toys

These space explorers aren't your average toys. They are LEGO® figures made entirely from a special type of space-grade metal that has been tested to make sure it won't interfere with anything on board. The trio are models of the ancient Roman god Jupiter, his wife Juno, and the scientist Galileo Galilei—who discovered the four largest moons of planet Jupiter.

Wow, this sure beats the view from inside our toy chest ...

Juno and Jupiter

The Juno spacecraft is on a mission to explore Jupiter and bring back more information about the largest planet in our solar system. It is hoped that this new knowledge should help scientists further develop ideas about the creation of giant planets and of our solar system. The onboard crew of three also have a further mission—to get more children interested in space travel.

Galileo Galilei

Ancient Romans thought Jupiter and Juno ruled over the other gods and goddesses.

The planet Jupiter and the Juno spacecraft circling around it.

Toys in space

These three special passengers aren't the first toys to go into space—several toys have been flown up to the International Space Station. Buzz Lightyear, from the movie *Toy Story*, has also spent 450 days in space, including a year aboard the International Space Station.

Along for the ride

As well as toys, there have been a number of interesting objects launched into space over the years. In 2018, billionaire Elon Musk launched a sports car into space aboard a rocket, and it is still speeding through our solar system.

FACT 80
A DAY IS LONGER THAN A YEAR ON VENUS

A day is how long a planet takes to spin all the way around. A year is how long it takes to circle the Sun. A Venus day is 243 Earth days— a year is only 225.

Slow spinner

Venus spins round veeeerry slowly compared with the other planets in our solar system, including Earth. This is why its days are so long. Weirdly, it doesn't always spin around at the same speed. Although it takes around 243 Earth days for Venus to turn all the way around and complete a day, the exact time can vary by up to seven minutes. Scientists are still not entirely sure why.

NEW DAY

LOADING ...

Odd one out

Venus also turns in the opposite direction of Earth and most other planets. And although its solid body takes 243 Earth days to turn all the way around, its atmosphere—the layers of gases around it—takes only four Earth days to complete the same rotation. Imagine the sky and the clouds on Earth spinning round 60 times faster than the planet under your feet—it's enough to make you dizzy!

Different days

Venus has the longest day of any planet in our solar system. A day on Mercury—the closest planet to the Sun—lasts a little under 2 ½ Earth days, and a day on Mars is just an hour longer than on Earth. Farther out, the other planets are much speedier spinners—a day on Jupiter is just 10 hours, the shortest of all. Saturn (11 hours), Uranus (17 hours), and Neptune (16 hours) aren't too far behind.

Round trip

The closer a planet is to the Sun, the shorter its journey around it. Mercury, the closest planet to the Sun, completes this loop in just 88 Earth days—giving it the shortest year of all our solar system's planets. A 12-year-old on Earth would be 52 years old if they lived on Mercury! And the longest year? That would be Neptune, where a year is 59,800 Earth days—or just under 164 Earth years.

I'm only six months old on Neptune!

YOU WEIGH LESS ON MARS THAN ON EARTH

No, the scale isn't just broken! Your weight is how much matter is in your body—your mass—multiplied by the force of gravity. Mars has less gravity than Earth, so you weigh less there.

But I wasn't even trying to lose weight!

What is gravity?

Gravity is the force that pulls you down to the ground on Earth so you don't float off into the sky. It is the same force that keeps the Moon circling around the Earth, and the planets circling around the Sun. It's also the force that holds galaxies together. Hmm, yep, gravity plays a pretty important part in the universe!

Changing weight

Someone who weighs 45kg (100lb) on Earth would weigh only 17kg (38lb) on Mars. Head to the Moon and their weight would drop even farther—right down to 7kg (17lb). That's about the same weight as a small dog on Earth! But head to giant Jupiter and it's a different story ... the same person would weigh around 2 ½ times as much as they do on Earth.

Weight on Earth

Even on Earth, your weight isn't exactly the same everywhere on the planet. Gravity is a bit stronger in some places on the Earth's surface, so without your mass changing you weigh more there. Your weight doesn't change anywhere near as much as it would if you went to a different planet altogether, but it's something that most of us have a much greater chance of experiencing!

We need gravity

Our bodies have evolved on Earth to work in our planet's level of gravity. When astronauts are aboard spacecraft, without the effect of gravity, their bodies struggle to stay healthy. Floating above the ground looks like great fun, but it takes so little effort that it's really bad for us. Astronauts' bones and muscles waste away when they are not used to work against gravity.

NEPTUNE'S MOON TRITON HAS ICE VOLCANOES

The ice volcanoes shoot out what scientists believe is a mixture of liquid nitrogen, methane, and dust. This instantly freezes and then snows back down to the surface.

Er, this moon looks a bit cold.

Brrr ... chilly!

It's so incredibly cold on Triton—the surface temperature is -391 °F (-235 °C)—that nitrogen and methane are both usually frozen solid. On Earth, they are usually gases and have to be made very, very cold before they even turn liquid, let alone solid.

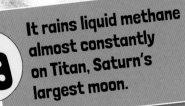

FACT 83 It rains liquid methane almost constantly on Titan, Saturn's largest moon.

Pepperoni moon

Io, one of Jupiter's moons, has the most volcanic activity of any object in our solar system. Its surface is covered with hundreds of exploding volcanoes—from far away, it looks a bit like a pepperoni pizza! These volcanoes can shoot jets up to 400 km (250 miles) into the atmosphere, in eruptions so violent that they can be seen by large telescopes on Earth around 630 million km (391 million miles) away.

Not the most appetizing-looking pizza ...

People used to think that the dark patches on the Moon were oceans, like those on Earth.

Mercury and the Moon

Even when a planet or moon no longer has active volcanoes, scientists can tell from clues on its surface whether it once did. Mercury's and the Moon's long-extinct volcanoes have left the remains of their huge lava flows that cooled and turned solid. These show up as dark plains on both their surfaces. The Moon also has large bumps on its surface, called lunar domes, which scientists think were made by lava erupting and cooling slowly in that spot.

Volcanoes on Mars

Millions of years ago, Mars used to have the solar system's largest active volcanoes, and the biggest of all was Olympus Mons. Although it is now long dead, it is still visible on Mars's surface. Olympus Mons is over three times the size of Earth's tallest mountain. In fact, it is so large that if you stood at the top you wouldn't even know you were on a mountain. The mountain slopes would stretch to the horizon and then be hidden by the curve of the planet.

FACT 84

JUPITER AND SATURN MAY HAVE DIAMOND RAIN

Scientists believe that it may rain down diamonds during storms on Jupiter and Saturn. The biggest diamonds would be around 1 cm (0.4 inches) across—big enough for a nice ring!

How to make diamonds

Do you want to become super-rich? Well, first, you should pick up a cow and head to Saturn or Jupiter. Next, wait for a lightning storm. When your cow passes wind, the methane gas will turn into a sooty form of carbon. The soot will fall back down through the planet's deep atmosphere. As it goes, it will be crushed into diamonds, which are just another form of carbon. Ta da!

FACT 85

Beyond our solar system, there is a planet twice the size of Earth which scientists think may be almost entirely made of diamond.

Is space the future of diamond mining?

Diamond seas

Scientists think that once these solid diamonds are formed, they move farther into the planet and eventually become liquid. This would create a liquid sea around the planet's core. Saturn and Jupiter are both gas giants, so their composition is very different to Earth. They look solid from far away but they are mostly made of squashed gases around a small solid or liquid core.

Space mining

Precious gems are big business on Earth—and, in the future, maybe even beyond Earth! The idea is that spacecraft could travel to other planets in our solar system, carrying robot mining ships that are able to collect the diamonds there. The spacecraft would then bring them back to Earth, to make some genuinely out-of-this-world jewels!

Odd weather

In the last 25 years or so, scientists have started exploring all the weird and wonderful planets outside our solar system. These are called exoplanets—and boy, do they have some strange weather of their own! On one planet, it snows rocks and on another it rains burning-hot glass sideways—you wouldn't want to get caught out in that, even with an umbrella. Yikes!

SATURN'S RINGS SOMETIMES DISAPPEAR

Around every 15 years, a trick of the sunlight makes it look to us on Earth as if Saturn's rings have vanished! The last time this happened was in 2009—keep your eyes out for next time ...

Thin rings

Saturn's rings are enormous, big enough to stretch around a planet 764 times bigger than Earth. But they are also very thin—scientists think that in some places they are just 10 m (30 ft) wide. Even at their thickest point the rings are only 1 km (0.6 miles) across, which an average person could walk in around 10 minutes.

FACT 87 One of Saturn's moons has a ridge around the middle, making it look like a giant walnut shell. Scientists think it formed when the moon absorbed some of Saturn's rings.

But I like my rings, I don't want them to disappear!

Disappearing trick

As Saturn moves around the Sun, it sometimes turns its rings edge-on to Earth. The rings are so thin that in a small telescope it looks like they've disappeared altogether! Four hundred years ago, this sight puzzled Galileo, one of the greatest space scientists of all time. Having first spotted the rings in 1610, he was very confused when they seemed to vanish again within two years. For a short time, he even stopped studying Saturn!

But ... the rings were right there! Weren't they?

Closer look

Saturn's rings are a wonderful sight, but do you know what they're made of? Dust, rock, and ice. Hmm, not quite as glamorous as they seem from a distance ... The pieces that make up the rings vary in size, from a grain of sand to a large-ish house. The rings speed round and round Saturn at great speed. It looks like Saturn has seven rings, but each of these is split up into smaller rings— called ringlets.

Neptune and its rings

Not so special

Saturn is not the only planet in our solar system to have rings surrounding it. In fact, all the other giant planets in our solar system—Jupiter, Uranus, and Neptune—have similar rings. Saturn's are famous for being the biggest and by far the most impressive sight, though. The other planets' rings are much darker and so cannot easily be seen from Earth.

THE MOON IS FALLING TOWARD US!

The Moon has been free-falling toward the Earth for billions of years. But don't panic! It is being pulled sideways at the same time, so it doesn't actually get closer to Earth.

Earth's gravity

What keeps you on Earth's surface instead of floating through the sky and out into space? That's right, it's gravity. The Earth's gravity constantly pulls you toward its middle—and you and the Moon have that in common! It is the reason that the Moon circles around and around Earth, rather than whizzing off into space.

Sideways pull

Aaarrrrghhh, I'm falling!

Gravitational pull toward Earth

We've been over this, you're always falling ...

At high speed

If you drop a ball from your hand, it will fall straight down to the ground. But if you throw a ball hard straight ahead of you, and there is nothing in the way, it will travel through the air for a while and then fall downward until it eventually lands on the ground. The Moon is moving at high speed around the Earth, so the downward pull of gravity isn't the only force acting on it.

Falling around Earth

Now imagine if you could throw the ball really fast. It would take a long time to drop down to Earth. If you could throw it superhumanly fast, it would never fall to the ground but just keep moving around and around the Earth. This is what the Moon is doing! It is far enough away, and moves fast enough that it never crashes down to Earth's surface, but instead constantly falls in a curve around Earth.

Balancing act

If the Moon moved a lot faster than it does, it would break away entirely from the pull of Earth's gravity and fly off into space. If it moved much slower, it would be dragged all the way down by Earth's gravity and crash into our planet. The perfect balance between the Moon's speed and its gravity means that it stays in constant orbit around the Earth.

When rockets are launched into space, their speed is set to either join or escape Earth's orbit.

FACT 89
SUNSETS ON MARS ARE BLUE

On Earth, we are used to blue sky in the day and red-orange sunsets in the evening. On Mars, it's the other way around! It has a red sky in the day, with blue sunsets.

YOU CAN SEE MARS IN THE NIGHT SKY WITHOUT A TELESCOPE FOR MOST OF THE YEAR.

Blue skies

On Earth, the particles that make up our atmosphere—the layers of gases that surround our planet—partly block the Sun's light and scatter it around the sky. They are much better at scattering blue light than red light, so we see this blue light spread across the sky. This means that most of the time on Earth our sky looks blue.

Look, the Sun's going down. Must be home time!

Reddish sunset

At sunset, Earth's position has moved so that the Sun is now on the horizon rather than appearing high in the sky. The Sun's light now has to pass through so much of Earth's atmosphere that all the blue light is scattered away so that other shades can be seen. This is why sunsets on Earth have their beautiful golden-reddish-orange glow.

Yeah yeah the orange is pretty, but I prefer black and white!

Reddish skies

On Mars, things are a little different. Mars has lots and lots of dust in its atmosphere, which blocks all shades of light about the same amount. This dust is reddish, which makes it absorb the blue light and scatter the red light, so on Mars the sky is usually red.

Blue sunset

The reason that Mars has blue sunsets is to do with these dust particles, too. Looking at the Sun from Mars, there is actually always a blue halo around it, but it is only when the Sun appears on the horizon that its light passes through all the dust and the blue halo is easy to see.

IF YOU PUT SATURN IN A GIANT BATH, IT WOULD FLOAT

Y ou'd need to find a bathtub 60,000 km (38,000 miles) wide to give this a go, but it's true—Saturn is so light for its size that it would float on the surface of water.

> I am just so relaxed right now!

SATURN IS A SLIGHTLY SQUISHED CIRCLE SHAPE, WIDEST AROUND ITS MIDDLE.

Huge but light

Saturn is huge, big enough to fit 764 Earths inside it. But although it takes up so much space, the lightness of the materials that make it up means that it doesn't have very much mass for its size at all. Another way to say this is that it has low density. Because it has a lower density than liquid water, Saturn should float on the surface of water, just like a beach ball or a boat does.

Gassy giant

What makes Saturn so light, when it's so huge? In a word, gas. Saturn is a very different sort of planet to Earth—while Earth is made of relatively heavy solids and liquids, Saturn is mostly made of gases, which are much lighter. In fact, Saturn's main gases are especially light ones—hydrogen and helium, the lightest elements in existence (as far as we know).

Helium is lighter than air, so balloons filled with helium float.

The Cassini spacecraft exploring Saturn and its moons.

Mysterious middle

Scientists think Saturn has either a liquid or a solid core in its middle, but they're still not sure exactly which it is. Saturn is a long way from Earth—at its closest to us, it is still 1.2 billion km (746 million miles) away. That's over 3,000 times farther away than the Moon! A spacecraft called Cassini spent over 10 years exploring around Saturn, but there's still a lot for us to learn about the planet.

Tricky test

Can you imagine trying to float a giant swirling ball of gas in a bathtub almost 1,000 times bigger than Earth? It's pretty tricky without a solid surface because we can't even know for sure where Saturn starts and finishes! Well, "floating Saturn" shows us the very real truth that it's less dense than liquid water—but, in reality, it probably wouldn't work quite as well as a nice rubber duck!

BILLIONS OF PLANETS DON'T CIRCLE ANY STAR

"Rogue planets" are free-floating planets that have broken away from a star and wander through the universe. They're the rebel runaways of the planet world!

I'm a rebel without a star!

Breaking free

When new solar systems are forming, it's absolute chaos. All sorts of materials swirl around a star in a packed, top-speed confusion, whizzing past and crashing into each other as they go. Most scientists believe that at these times many planets are thrown out of the mix with such force that they leave the system altogether and speed off alone through space.

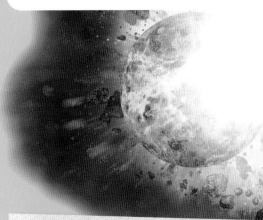
Violent crashes may send rogue planets spinning off alone into space

The red dot in this photo is the rogue planet PSO J318.5–22.

Giant runaways

Rogue planets are big. Waaay bigger than Earth. In fact, the smallest rogue planets are around the size of Jupiter—which is our solar system's largest planet by far, big enough to fit 1,300 Earths inside it. There aren't just the odd few of them wandering around space either—scientists think there may be twice as many rogue planets as there are stars in the universe!

Tricky to spot

Despite their huge size, rogue planets are actually very hard for scientists to spot. They do not give off any light, and as they aren't near to a star they can't be seen interfering with the light it gives off—which is how scientists can see many star-circling planets. When rogue planets pass in front of far-off stars, scientists can see the effect of this and work out that they are there, but it is very rare.

Rogue life?

We get our light and heat from the Sun, our nearest star. But rogue planets don't have a friendly nearby star to keep them nice and toasty-warm, so they are very cold. Not quite as cold as you may think, though. Rogue planets produce some heat of their own, maybe even enough to support life—although of a very different kind to anything on Earth ...

Hello!

FACT 92 JUPITER HAS A STORM BIGGER THAN EARTH

Jupiter's Great Red Spot is a huge, swirling storm that can easily be seen on the planet's surface. It has been going on for 350 years and Earth could fit inside it with room to spare.

Super sized

Jupiter is the biggest planet in our solar system by a very long way—all our solar system's other planets could fit inside it with room to spare! And scientists think this super-sized planet's equally super-sized storm has been raging since more than 100 years before the USA was founded! Earth's longest recorded storm, Hurricane John, back in 1994, lasted just 31 days.

A storm the size of Earth is "little?!"

Shrinking storm

Jupiter's Great Red Spot has shrunk to half the size it was when it was first seen. It looks like it's finally dying down after all this time, and scientists think that in 20 years' time we probably won't be able to see it from Earth at all. The thick clouds around Jupiter don't help, as they make it quite hard to see the planet's surface.

Other Great Spots

Neptune and Saturn also have their own "Great Spots," whirling storms that can be seen from Earth. They aren't as reliable as Jupiter's Great Red Spot, though—they seem to disappear and they sometimes appear again in other places on the planet. Saturn has different Great White Spots and Neptune has a Great Dark Spot but only about half the time.

The Little Red Spot

Jupiter has lots of storms whirling around all over its surface. The Little Red Spot is another storm on Jupiter that has been growing since it was first spotted in 2006. It formed when three smaller storms joined together, and it is now around the same size as Earth. So not that little after all!

Imagine if Earth's storms joined together.

A MAN'S ASHES ARE BURIED ON THE MOON

Dr. Eugene Shoemaker was a brilliant scientist who helped to train astronauts going to the Moon. After his death, some of his ashes were carried to the Moon in 1999 and remain there to this day.

Eugene Shoemaker and his wife, Carolyn, spotted comets that had never been recorded before.

Groundbreaking scientist

Shoemaker was a geologist, a scientist who studies rocks. He devoted his life to space, looking at the different objects—such as moons, comets, and planets—in our solar system and how they were formed. He was a world-renowned expert in craters on Earth, other planets, and the Moon, and he trained astronauts to explore the Moon's rocks and craters in a scientific way. He also discovered several comets, which are named after him.

Shoemaker could never join astronauts on the Moon—not during his lifetime, anyway.

Astronaut dreams

Shoemaker had a lifelong dream to travel into space—and, above all, to go to the Moon. He was all set to be the first geologist to ever walk on the Moon, but tests at NASA found that he had a health condition which meant it wasn't considered safe for him to go. Although he had an incredible, scientific career filled with important achievements and awards, he was always haunted by his now-impossible dream.

Craters and comets

Shoemaker had a rich life exploring craters all over the world, often with his wife and fellow scientist Carolyn Shoemaker. It was on such a trip to Australia that he sadly died in a car accident while driving to a remote crater. Shortly before Shoemaker died, he said, "Not going to the Moon ... has been the biggest disappointment in life." But, as we know, his friends and family would put that right in his death.

Finally at peace

Shoemaker's ashes were carried to their final resting place on the Moon in a capsule etched with pictures of Comet Hale-Bopp, the last comet that he ever saw with his wife, and a quotation from Shakespeare's play *Romeo and Juliet*. Although some people have paid to launch their remains into space, Shoemaker is the only person buried anywhere else beyond Earth. His wife said, "We will always know when we look at the Moon, that he is there."

The quote on Shoemaker's ashes capsule reads:

**And, when he shall die
Take him and cut him out in little stars
And he will make the face of heaven so fine
That all the world will be in love with night
And pay no worship to the garish sun.**

FACT 94 GALAXIES CAN EAT EACH OTHER

Big galaxies crash into each other every 9 billion years or so. When this happens, they sometimes swallow up and merge with the other galaxy in order to grow larger. They're space cannibals!

Oi! Get your own gas!

Topping up

Galaxies need lots of gas to make new stars. Smaller galaxies have plenty of gas for this, but bigger galaxies are often running uncomfortably low. By merging with smaller galaxies, these bigger galaxies can be sure that their gas levels are topped up and that they will be able to continue making new stars.

These two galaxies, known as the Mice Galaxies, because of their long "tails," are in the process of merging.

Large Magellanic
Cloud

Milky Way

Small Magellanic
Cloud

In certain parts of the world, you can see the Milky Way and the Large and Small Magellanic Clouds in the night sky.

The Milky Way

Our galaxy, the Milky Way, has already eaten 15 smaller galaxies—chomp! It is likely to eat another two small galaxies, the Large and Small Magellanic Clouds, within 4 billion years or so. The Milky Way is in a stage of its life as a galaxy where it is now easier to keep itself going by swallowing up other galaxies than by creating its own stars.

Big bad Andromeda?

But the Milky Way might not be top of the galaxy food chain ... Some scientists think that our galaxy will itself be swallowed up by the Andromeda galaxy in around 5 billion years. It depends on how big Andromeda really is—for a long time it was believed to be around twice the size of the Milky Way, but a recent study has found that it might actually be the same size.

Merging stars

It isn't only galaxies that crash into each other and merge into one. Stars do it too, with a "stellar collision" of this type happening somewhere in the universe once every 10,000 years. All types of stars can merge—one particularly strange mix is a Thorne–Żytkow object, where a neutron star and a red giant star crash and merge. What you get is a neutron star in the middle, surrounded by a red giant!

An artist's impression of two neutron stars merging.

THE ROTTEN EGG NEBULA SMELLS TERRIBLE

What's in a name? Well, for the Rotten Egg Nebula there's quite a bit of truth to it. It contains a lot of sulfur, which—when combined with other materials—smells like rotten eggs!

Gross!

What is a nebula?

A nebula is an enormous cloud of dust and gas in space. Some of them are areas where new stars are starting to form, and others are the remains flung out into space by a dying star. Either way, they exist in what we call interstellar space—areas of space in between star systems.

Faraway stink

Don't worry too much about catching a whiff of this space stinker—it's far enough from Earth that we can't smell it at all. The Rotten Egg Nebula is about 5,000 light years from Earth, meaning that it's so far away it takes light 5,000 years to travel that far. To give an idea of how far away that is, it takes light less than 1.5 seconds to travel between Earth and the Moon.

Big change

The Rotten Egg Nebula is interesting to scientists because it's going through a change that they are rarely able to see happening. A red giant star is in the process of dying and violently shedding its outer layers of gas and dust. This change takes around 2,000 years in total, which sounds like a long time but is a blink of an eye in space terms, so it's lucky for scientists to see it in action.

The Hubble telescope took this picture of the Horsehead Nebula.

THE WORD "NEBULA" COMES FROM THE LATIN WORD FOR "CLOUD."

Nebula names

The Rotten Egg Nebula does actually have a more polite name—it's also known as the Calabash Nebula. A calabash is a kind of vegetable that has a shape a bit like a bowling pin, which is sort of what this nebula looks like. Other nebula have names that describe what they look like, too—some of the spookiest are the Ghost, Skull, and Witch Head nebulae!

The Witch Head Nebula looks like a witch screaming into space—scary stuff!

FACT 96

THERE MAY BE UP TO 2 TRILLION GALAXIES

Scientists find it hard to agree on how many galaxies there are in the universe. Some think it's 200 million, a computer program said 500 million, and others believe there are far, far more.

The big questions

When scientists try to work out the answers to huge questions about space, such as "How many galaxies are there in the known universe?", they have to use the information that people have already gathered and use it to make predictions. Computer programs now help scientists to do this in more complex and accurate ways than were possible in the past.

It's out of this world, man!

Seen and unseen

Scientists got to the figure of 2 trillion galaxies by creating models in a computer program, based on the Hubble telescope's 20-year collection of images. The Hubble telescope shows us more of space than ever, but scientists believe that only 10% of the known universe's galaxies are visible to us now. The figure of 2 trillion galaxies takes this into account, so it's a lot higher than the number of galaxies that have actually been seen.

Computers are a huge part of space science, from controlling missions to running simulations with data.

Galaxy shapes

The galaxies that we can see at the moment don't all look the same. Most are in the shape of a spiral or an egg, but some have no particular shape at all—they just look like a vague assortment of stars, gas, and dust spread out in all directions. Our galaxy, the Milky Way, is a spiral galaxy.

Sombreros and tadpoles

Scientists have had great fun naming some of the galaxies that we've discovered so far. There is the Sombrero Galaxy, the Tadpole Galaxy, and the Sunflower Galaxy, for a start. The Milky Way's name comes from an Ancient Greek myth about the goddess Hera spraying milk across the sky. In China, it is called the Silver River and in the Kalahari Desert in Southern Africa it is known as the Backbone of Night.

The Sombrero Galaxy is named after the wide Mexican hat that it looks like!

FACT 97
A BLACK HOLE COULD STRETCH YOU LIKE SPAGHETTI

Don't get too close to the edge of a black hole! If it's a smallish one, its gravity will pull hardest on the closest part of you and streeeeetch it away from the rest.

Spaghettification

This all sounds terrifying, but at least it gives us a great word—spaghettification! This describes how an object falling into a black hole is stretched, and sometimes ripped apart, by the force of gravity. An object spaghettified by a black hole would be trapped inside it, stretching out farther and farther for ever and ever.

It's one way to grow taller!

FACT 98
White holes, the opposite of black holes, should be possible, but we haven't found any yet. They would only give out light and matter, nothing would be able to enter them.

This illustration shows a glowing stream of material from a star as it is sucked in by a black hole.

No escape

A black hole has very strong gravity, which gets much stronger the closer you get to it. Once you have been sucked into the black hole, you can't escape it—no matter or light can. That's why black holes are invisible.

Spaghettifying stars

It's not just humans who are at risk of this spaghettification—we know that it happens to stars. In fact, we've seen black holes tearing stars apart in this way! Stars are only at risk if they stray too close to the edge of a black hole, though. This is called the black hole's "event horizon," and it's like the edge of a waterfall—the closest anything can get without being pulled down into it.

Exploring a black hole

There may be no escape from a black hole, but if you'd like to at least be able to have a look around inside rather than be totally spaghettified, make sure to pick a big one. The gravity of very large black holes is enough to suck you in whole. Most galaxies have the largest type of black hole—our galaxy, the Milky Way, has one called Sagittarius A in its middle.

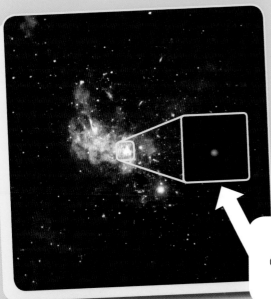

Scientists think this blue dot was a flash of light, caused when an asteroid fell into Sagittarius A and was torn apart.

THERE COULD BE AN INFINITE NUMBER OF UNIVERSES

Some of the most cutting-edge ideas about space can sound like something out of science fiction. To make sense of the strangeness of space, scientists have to open their minds to all sorts of possibilities.

Rules don't apply

Scientists are learning more about space every day, but sometimes instead of this answering any big questions it just opens up lots more new questions! We know that lots of things about space don't fit in exactly with our rules for how things work on Earth, so scientists have to think creatively about the different models that could make our universe work the way it seems to.

Not alone?

One of the most out-there ideas about our universe is simply that it's not the only one. Most scientists until now have worked on the assumption that nothing else exists beyond or alongside our universe—that our universe is literally everything. But until around 100 years ago, we thought that our galaxy was the only one in existence, whereas now we know it's just one of billions upon billions ...

Multiverse theory

The idea that there is more than one universe is known as the "multiverse" theory. Within this idea, there are lots of possibilities for how these multiple universes might be arranged. Some scientists have thought about them as bubbles within bubbles, some as a patchwork quilt stretching on forever, some as slices of bread side by side within a larger loaf.

> Could our universe be just one patch in the quilt of existence?!

> That's a lot of universes!

Infinite universes

If we describe something as infinite, it means it is never-ending. One version of the multiverse theory is that there are infinite universes. This is based on the understanding that there is no limit to how much space and time exists—in this case, why would we be limited to one universe, or any number of universes? These other universes may be invisible to us, but that doesn't necessarily mean they don't exist. Strange to think about!

WE MIGHT HAVE FOUND ALIENS WITHOUT REALIZING

One of the biggest questions about the universe is "Are we alone?" The answer? We still don't know. Scientists don't think they've found alien life, but they admit they might not recognize it if they saw it.

Seeing in space

It can be tricky for scientists to see exactly what's going on far off in space. When things are very distant from Earth, it's not like looking at something through binoculars on Earth. They can't always get a clear, detailed picture of what they're trying to see, so it might be tricky to see signs of life. Sometimes scientists can't actually "see" an object at all, but they know it's there from how it affects its surroundings.

Hey ... HEY ... I'm over here!

122

NASA IS CURRENTLY RUNNING MISSIONS TO TRY TO FIND ALIEN LIFE IN SPACE.

Unfamiliar beings

It can be hard to imagine something completely outside your own experiences. When scientists look for proof of life elsewhere in the universe, they are searching for evidence based on their knowledge of the needs and qualities of living things on Earth. But alien life might be so different to any sort of life we're familiar with that scientists are missing the very different signs of its existence.

Simple life

When we imagine alien life, we often think of creatures fairly similar to ourselves—they may look different, they might be bright green with huge pulsating brains, but they are intelligent life forms. Actually, many planets and moons may be able to support some kind of simple life, like the bacteria we have on Earth, but the chances of finding intelligent life is far lower.

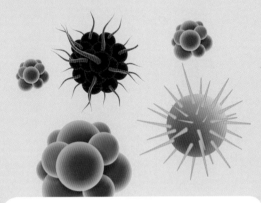

Alien life may be simple, tiny creatures like bacteria—or something else entirely!

Extreme Earth

Scientists have found living creatures surviving in conditions on Earth so extreme that we thought it was impossible for any life to exist there. They have discovered simple life forms called microbes living in burning-hot pure acid in Ethiopia's Danakil Depression, one of the hottest places on Earth. Studying these extreme-living microbes helps us understand how and where alien life might be found in space, in conditions where humans couldn't survive.

The Danakil Depression might look like somewhere on another planet, but it's right here on Earth!

95% OF THE UNIVERSE IS MISSING

Less than 5% of the universe is made of matter and energy as we understand it and can see it. The rest of it is invisible dark matter and dark energy. Gulp.

Missing matter

Scientists have realized that in space lots of things aren't quite adding up ... For instance, galaxies are spinning so quickly that the gravity from their visible matter shouldn't be strong enough to hold them together. They should have torn themselves apart a long time ago, but they haven't. Scientists think this is because they have more matter, which is invisible to us—they call this dark matter.

95% Dark matter

5% Atomic matter

Spinning so quickly means we have to hold on tight!

Dark energy

Dark energy is even more mysterious than dark matter—and scientists think it makes up over 70% of the universe. While scientists have some ideas about what dark matter might be—strange and not-yet-seen particles—they struggle a lot more to explain dark energy. The reason they think it exists is because the universe is growing and pulling galaxies farther apart, so there must be a greater force acting against the gravity that holds galaxies together.

Astronomical voids

There are huge areas in space where there are no or very few galaxies—scientists call them astronomical voids. But what looks like empty space to us might be something that we just don't understand yet. There is a giant Cold Spot in the universe, a cooler area that scientists think has many of these voids, and one idea is that it could be the spot where our universe crashed into another one!

Still learning

Essentially, dark matter and dark energy are what scientists think bridge the gap between what we have measured in space and how we see the universe behaving. We are still only just starting to understand many things about space, and how its strange forces and structures work. Many ideas that scientists have today might turn out to be wrong or to be only one part of the answer—that's how science develops.

Glossary

asteroid A small rocky object made up of material left over from the birth of the solar system.

astronomical void A vast area of space containing very few galaxies or none at all.

atmosphere A shell of gases kept around a planet, star, or other object by its gravity.

Big Bang The way in which many scientists believe the universe began—a huge, hot explosion that expanded out all the matter in the universe from one tiny point. Since this explosion, the universe has continued growing outward and is still doing so today.

black hole A superdense point in space, usually formed by a collapsed core of a giant star. A black hole's gravity is so powerful that even light cannot escape from it.

comet A chunk of rock and ice from the edge of the solar system.

dark energy An unknown form of energy that many scientists think exists throughout the universe, acting in opposition to gravity and causing the universe to expand faster and faster over time.

dark matter A strange, invisible substance that forms most of the mass in the universe.

dwarf planet A world, orbiting a star, that looks like a planet but does not meet certain criteria needed to make it a true planet.

exoplanet A planet orbiting a star outside our solar system.

galaxy A large system of stars, gas, and dust with anything from millions to trillions of stars.

gravity A natural force created around objects with mass, which draws other objects toward them.

International Space Station An artificial satellite that circles around Earth with astronauts from all over the world living on board and carrying out scientific experiments.

Kuiper Belt A ring of small icy worlds directly beyond the orbit of Neptune. Pluto is the largest known Kuiper Belt Object.

light year The distance light travels in a year—about 9.5 trillion km (5.9 trillion miles).

magnetar A small, very dense, strongly magnetic type of neutron star.

meteor The glowing path of a small piece of rock or other matter that has entered Earth's atmosphere. It appears as a fast-moving streak of light in the night sky, and is also known as a "shooting star."

meteorite A solid piece of an object from space—such as an asteroid, meteoroid, or comet—that has fallen to the Earth's surface.

meteoroid A small rocky or metallic object moving through space.

microgravity Very weak gravity, as you would find inside a spacecraft circling around Earth.

Milky Way Our home galaxy, a spiral with a bar across its core. Our solar system is about 28,000 light years from the monster black hole at its heart.

Moon Earth's closest companion in space, a ball of rock that orbits Earth every 27.3 days. Most other planets in the solar system have moons of their own.

nebula A cloud of gas or dust floating in space. Nebulae are the raw material used to make stars.

neutron star The core of a supermassive star, left behind by a supernova explosion and collapsed to the size of a city. Many neutron stars are also pulsars.

observatory A building or room that contains a telescope or other scientific equipment used to study space.

Oort Cloud A spherical (ball-shaped) shell of sleeping comets, surrounding all of the solar system out to a distance of about two light years.

orbit A fixed path taken by one object in space around another because of the effect of gravity.

planet A world, orbiting a star, which has enough mass and gravity to pull itself into a ball-like shape, and clear space around it of other large objects.

protostar A pressurized cloud of gas that is on its way to becoming a true star, but can still fail and become a brown dwarf if it can't pull in enough gas as it forms.

pulsar A fast-spinning neutron star whose intense magnetic field forces its radiation into two narrow beams that sweep around the sky like a lighthouse. From Earth, a pulsar appears as a quickly flashing star.

quasar A distant, active object in space that has a very bright core and gives out a huge amount of energy.

red dwarf A small, faint star with a cool red surface and less than half the mass of the Sun.

red giant A huge, brilliant (very bright) star near the end of its life, with a cool, red surface. Red giants are stars that have used up the fuel supply in their core and are going through big changes in order to keep shining for a little longer.

rocket A vehicle that drives itself forward through a controlled chemical explosion and can therefore travel in the vacuum of space. Rockets are the only practical way to launch spacecraft and satellites.

rocky planet An Earth-sized or smaller planet, made up mostly of rocks and minerals, sometimes with a thin outer layer of gas and water.

satellite Any object orbiting a planet. Moons are natural satellites made of rock and ice. Artificial (man-made) satellites are machines in orbit around Earth.

solar system The eight planets (including Earth) and their moons, and other objects such as asteroids, which orbit around the Sun.

spacecraft A vehicle that travels into space.

spiral galaxy A galaxy with a hub of old yellow stars (sometimes crossed by a bar) surrounded by a flattened disk of younger stars, gas, and dust. Bright newborn stars make a spiral pattern across the disk.

starquake A violent shaking and ripping of the crust of a type of star called a magnetar, similar in some ways to an earthquake on Earth.

supernova An enormous explosion marking the death of a star much more massive than the Sun.

telescope A device that collects light or other radiations from space and uses them to create a bright, clear image. Telescopes can use either a lens or a mirror to collect light.

white dwarf The dense, burned-out core of a star like the Sun, collapsed to the size of the Earth but still intensely hot.